Walks in t...
and th...

*Jim Manson with two of his most faithful
walking companions.*

The Devil's Beef Tub.

Walks in the
MOFFAT HILLS
AND THE LOWTHERS

Jim Manson

CAMERON & HOLLIS
Moffat

Published by Cameron & Hollis
the publishing imprint of Cameron Books
PO Box 1, Moffat, Dumfriesshire DG10 9SU, Scotland
Telephone: 01683 220808   Fax: 01683 220012

Edited by Jill Hollis
Designed by Ian Cameron

Maps by Jill Hollis

Typeset in New Baskerville by Cameron Books, Moffat

Acknowledgements
I would like to thank the following for their kind help in writing this book: on the bird
life, Jock Dicerbo and Bobby Smith, ornithologists and authors; Alastair Scott, fellow
member of Moffat Mountain Rescue Team for his guidance on the fauna; my
publisher, Jill Hollis, for her patience and hard work during the editing of this book.
Also my wife, Maureen, who did the research on the flora, laboriously typed out the
manuscript and encouraged me to get it all into print.

The text describing the walks in this book is based on articles originally written for the
Dumfries and Galloway Standard.

Photographs by: Drew Armstrong, pp.16, 36 (top); Jim Manson, pp.9, 14-15, 36
(bottom), 45, 52 (bottom), 68 (top and bottom), 69, 77, 90, 110, 112; Andy Newlands,
10, 52 (top), 101, 105; Jill Hollis and Ian Cameron, front cover, pp.2, 10, 17, 26, 57, 62,
74, 113; photograph on p.1 by courtesy of the Dumfries and Galloway Standard.

FOR MY GRANDCHILDREN – KATIE, DREW, LAUREN, DEBORAH, EVE AND FINLAY

Contents

Safety in the Hills

Although the border hills are not as high as those found further north, walkers should treat them with respect. Bad weather can turn them into a very exposed and inhospitable environment.

Unlike the fells of the Lake District, the hills of Ettrick, Moffatdale and the Lowthers are not crossed by many paths. So walkers should always carry a map and compass and be competent in their use. Mist can descend very suddenly, making navigation difficult.

One particular hazard can arise in wintry conditions. After heavy snowfalls, or where drifting has happened, cornices can build up along the edges of steep drops, disguising the edge of solid ground, and avalanches can strike – just as in the Highlands. Take great care not to go too near the edge in these conditions, even on walks where I have recommended walking fairly close to the edge to get a good view. You should always be able to see solid ground beneath your feet when you do this.

Walkers should be suitably clothed in good, waterproof and windproof gear and carry spare clothing and plenty of food. Always leave word of your route and any possible detours you might take. If you are planning to stay overnight in the hills, and to leave your car parked where you start you walk, it is wise to leave word at the local police station so that rescue services can be alerted if your return is overdue.

Note on Maps

The Ordnance Survey maps required for use in conjunction with this book are numbers 73, 78 and 79. However, it can be a source of some annoyance that walks in the Moffat Hills tend to fall across two, or even three, maps. So if you are intending to make a habit of walking in this area, it is probably worth investing in the Southern Upland Way maps, which reproduce the O.S. grid in such a way that almost all the walks around Moffat appear on one sheet at a time. Only the Black Esk and Wamphray Glen walks fall outside its ambit.

The maps in this book are intended to accompany the text as rough guides to the shapes of the walks. They include only the more obvious landmarks (e.g. some of the larger burns, but not necessarily their tributaries) and should not be relied upon for navigation.

Times given for the walks include lunch breaks and pauses taken for breathers under the pretext of admiring the view.

Introduction

In recent years, a certain amount of concern has been expressed about the rapidly increasing numbers of people taking to British hills – numbers which in some places are testing the delicate relationship between landlord and walker to the limit. And let's be honest, the behaviour of some of the more recent devotees often leaves something to be desired. It bears remembering that the same hills we love to roam are also someone else's place of work, be it to herd sheep or tend grouse. Bear in mind that the area which encompasses Moffatdale, Ettrick and the Lowthers is essentially sheep country. Always close gates behind you, and I would ask any of you, who, like myself, like to take your dogs along, to keep them well under control. During the lambing season, it's probably better to leave them at home. That way, if you are late, you are at least sure of a welcome from one member of the family.

Some of the more critical, and frequently long in the tooth, bemoan the fact that they no longer have the hills to themselves. One has to admit that hill-goers, myself included, are just a wee bit on the possessive side. The sight of another walker is enough to raise the old blood pressure by a few points, and a group of walkers can bring on apoplexy. Sheep farmers will tell you that a sheep's worst enemy is another sheep. It's a bit that way with hillwalkers and climbers. They hate the sight of you when they spy you on the horizon, but the majority enjoy passing the time of day with you when you finally draw level.

While walking with some friends on the rough, high ground that lies just into the old county of Peebles, above the Devil's Beef Tub, it struck me that the area is not exactly overcrowded. Despite the fact that more people are now enjoying hill-walking, the hills and high moors of Annandale and Tweed, for example, see only the occasional passing walker or shepherd. Except for the ruins of the farm at Earlshaugh, the area is a vast tract of wild and glorious desolation. Apart from the odd sheep, deer and mountain hare, nothing moves over the boggy ground dissected by the Powskein and Whitehope burns as they snake their way through the knowes to feed the infant rivers Annan and Tweed. The skies above are the domain of the buzzard, raven and skylark. At times, the Edinburgh road can be seen, but not heard, at a comfortable distance.

In former times, the area saw a great deal more action than it does these days (*see* page 13). I don't suppose the Moss Troopers bothered about the laws of access when they rode out by moonlight to 'borrow' cattle. They were probably just exercising their freedom to roam.

Moffat in the 18th and 19th Centuries

Moffat's reputation as a spa was established relatively early. By 1657, the medicinal properties of the sulphureous waters of Moffat Well were sufficiently recognised for a grant to be made to erect an enclosure at Archbank, and in 1748 a second (chalybeate) well, Hartfell Spa, was discovered. By the 1780s, most of the houses dating from before 1760 had been rebuilt, and the High Street had been widened. However, it wasn't until the first half of the 19th century that the town began to draw to it large numbers of visitors, partly as a result of the opening of Beattock railway station in 1847. Several prominent physicians in Edinburgh and Glasgow, among them Dr William Johnstone, extolled the healing properties of the waters from the three spas at Garpol, Archbank and Hartfell, advocating treatment for any number of ills at the Moffat Spa. The numbers of visitors to the rural resort increased sharply, and the couthie citizens were not slow to recognise the business opportunity that presented itself.

The first large hotel, the Annandale Arms, was built in about 1783. (The Moffat House Hotel, designed by John Adams and built in 1762 was still a private house at this time.) In 1827, the building housing the Vapour and Mineral Baths (at the rear of the present town hall, which

Hartfell Spa.

Moffat in winter sunshine from the slopes of Upper Annandale.

was the Assembly Rooms) opened its doors, equipped with a supply of water piped in from the spa at Archbank, and in 1878, the colossal and luxuriously appointed Hydropathic Hotel was built on the hillside above the Old Edinburgh Road, with 300 bedrooms on five floors as well as its own vapour and mineral baths. Access to the town for the general public was further improved by the laying of a railway track between Moffat and Beattock operated by the Caledonian Railway Company and paid for by the issue of £16,000 worth of £10 shares.

The boom of Moffat as a spa town came to a rather abrupt end, in common with many other spas across Europe. By the 1920s, seaside holidays were fast gaining popularity over breaks in country lodgings, and in 1921 the grandiose Hydro was (somewhat mysteriously) destroyed by fire. Not a trace of it remains.

Today's times seem placid by comparison with Moffat's past, but the town's High Street is always busy. Once a focus of sheep sales, the little town now depends largely on tourism, and its restaurants, hotels and guest houses give good service to the walker, making it an ideal centre for those wishing to spend a few days or more in the hills. From spring to autumn, tourists throng its shops, pubs, restaurants and ice-cream parlours, all under the watchful eye of the Moffat Ram high on his pedestal.

The Moffat Water Valley

Not all the visitors to Moffat in the 1800s and 1900s came to the wee town to take the waters. Some preferred to travel up the Moffat Water valley in the numerous charabancs which left the various hostelries each morning and journeyed up as far as St Mary's Loch where they no doubt slaked their thirst and fed the inner man.

The Moffat Water valley, originally gouged out by an immense glacier which apparently ran from St Mary's Loch to way beyond Moffat is, in my opinion, one of the most beautiful valleys in the south of Scotland. As it snakes its way between the high hills on each side, out through copses of shimmering birch and sturdy rowan, the Moffat Water luxuriates in a valley second to none. It rises, up near the old Selkirk border, at 550 metres, and, as it meanders its way west towards its meeting with the Annan, it is fed from its right by the Tail Burn (flowing out of Loch Skeen), the Carrifran, Blackhope and Craigie burns, and on the left by the Bodesbeck, Sailfoot, Selcoth, Crofthead and Cornal waters.

In the 19th century, such was the respect in which the hills of Moffatdale were held that they were known in travel books of the day as the 'Southern Alps'. Many of the visitors would stop then, as now, to admire the Grey Mare's Tail plunging hundreds of feet down into the Giant's Grave. The bolder in spirit would climb the steep path, just as thousands do each year today, to view little Loch Skeen nestling high above the valley. The wee loch was in fact formed when the glacier, following the courses of both the Tail and Midlaw burns, gouged out the defile which cradles the falls, deposited spoil from its lateral moraines which hold back the water, and created the basin for the loch. In those days, it was well worth a visit for fishers: a fair day's catch weighed 12 to 18 lbs. It's a different story today.

Walter Scott was so impressed by the majesty of the Tail that, in spite of getting so bogged down there that his horse was up to its belly in soft ground, he celebrated it in his poem, *Marmion* (which some of us remember repeating parrot-fashion at school).

Before reaching the Grey Mare's Tail, the intrepid charabanc traveller would have come to Craigieburn, a favourite stop for Robert Burns on his way to sample the delights of Auld Reekie. It was seemingly here that he wrote the words, 'We are no fu', we're nae that fu'.' He must have had quite a night.

Further on from Craigieburn you come to Shortwoodend, nestling down to the right among the trees just off the road. Not so long ago this was a youth hostel. The men's dormitory, once a byre and hayloft, was a small building separate from the main part. This was the first youth hostel I ever visited and, at the tender age of nine, I was the sole occupant of the men's dormitory. I remember feeling distinctly ostracised and quite perturbed by the quietness of the surroundings – something I hadn't experienced before. On the second night, I talked myself into the main building.

Opposite the car park at the Tail rises the mass of Bodesbeck Ridge, with Herman Law, Bellcraig and Bodesbeck Law forming a magnificent day's ridge wandering. Mind you, Moffat Water must have been a pretty frightening place during the Killing Times; what with the superstitious locals and the fugitives creeping about in the hills, and flashing lights making all kinds of signal at dead of night. There's an account of a lay preacher by the name of William Moffat of Hartfell, who was keen on conducting blanket preachings for the followers of the Covenant in the hills surrounding the valley. He had one particularly narrow escape from the dragoons which he later put down to the intervention of divine providence. In the middle of his sermon, he and his followers noticed that a flock of sheep grazing on a nearby hillside had suddenly started across the hill as if startled by something. Almost at once, a troop of dragoons appeared, riding at full tilt towards their prey. The Covenanters fled in the opposite direction, but the dragoons were soon gaining on them, when a thick mist suddenly rolled silently across the hillside between the fugitives and their pursuers. The Covenanters heard the thud of the hoof beats as the troops rode past them, oblivious to their presence.

Travellers going on up the valley would no doubt have set their horses' heads to the long steep pull over the pass at Birkhill. Here, during the Killing Times, 'Bloody Clavers' had two young Covenanters shot at the door of the inn. In more peaceful times, travellers such as Robert Burns and Sir Walter Scott (on his way to and from Drumlanrig) would rest and take food and drink. Some were given lodgings for the night.

Charabanc travellers would finish their journey at the Tibbie Shiels Inn at St Mary's Loch. James Hogg, the Ettrick Shepherd and local bard, spent many a night in the company of the landlady after whom the inn is named and enjoyed frequent drams under her roof. She said of him: 'He was a gey sensible man for a' the nonsense he wrote'.

The tourist and hillwalker may nowadays have replaced the itinerant writer, poet or bold explorer, but the spell cast by the beauty and grandeur of Moffat Water remains as powerful as ever.

Moffat and its Environs

The rich history of the hills around Moffat can be touched upon only briefly here, but a bit of background gives you something to ponder as you walk through what is now a very sparsely populated landscape. There have been times when the area was far from tranquil.

In the first century AD, a tribe called the Selgovae lived around what is now Durisdeer, and it was to keep them under control that the Romans first built forts and roads in the area. Over in Annandale, the road along which the Roman legions travelled north is thought to have run along the valley leading towards the floor of the Devil's Beef Tub, out over the top to the north and up into Tweedsmuir. Overlooking the Tub, high on Eric Stane Hill, stood a Roman watchtower. Later the Picts and the Cymri established settlements in this region: signs of their earthworks are still clearly visible in the area of the Beef Tub, Newton Farm and Fingland at Wamphray.

In the thirteenth and fourteenth centuries, both the English and the Scottish armies moved through these wild hills. Robert the Bruce rode out of Annandale, no doubt with an army largely consisting of local men, on his way to Scone to be crowned. After the Scots' momentous victory over the English at Bannockburn in 1314, the Scottish king made a gift of vast tracts of land in Moffatdale and Annandale to his staunch ally, Sir James Douglas.

Up to the mid sixteenth century, the lands of Annanwater were known as Annerdaill and, I regret to say, the residents as 'Annerdaill thieves'. Talking of thieves, that period saw more than its fair share of violent and criminal activity. Because of the continual incursions into the border lands by national armies, the local population showed little enthusiasm for tilling the soil. It seemed more sensible and vastly more profitable to ride over into England and steal some cattle. Local families, among them the Scotts, Elliots, Maxwells, Moffats, Johnstones and Jardines, all became adept in the art of reiving. To give the Reivers their due, blood was shed only as a last resort, but they had efficient ways of extracting money from their weaker neighbours.

The Moss Troopers, as some of the cross-border raiders became known, travelled by night, picking their way through the knowes and bogs astride small hill ponies through Annandale, the Debateable Lands and on to the English Marches. Moonlight was their friend and indeed the motto of the Scotts of Harden was 'We'll have moonlight again'. Anybody who didn't take their fancy was dumped in the Falla Moss. In the eighteenth century, when parts of this boggy area were drained, fourteen bodies of men from Cromwell's army were found.

Near the end of a December day on the Crown of Scotland.

Looking over Loch Skeen towards Donald's Cleuch.

Stock seized south of the border was often hidden in the huge natural corral known as the Devil's Beef Tub, or the 'Earl of Annandale's Larder', which drops spectacularly away from the A701 just north of Moffat. Up on the Gallow Hill to the east stands the site of the bale fire which was lit by the residents as a warning when the English were approaching.

With the dawning of the seventeenth century came the Covenanters, and numbers of the old reiving families took to the religious struggle like fish to water. Reiving had become a rather squalid occupation, so many were now looking for a good cause to which they could give their militant support. The trouble all started when Charles I tried to introduce the Episcopal Church (an equivalent of the Anglican Communion in England) into Scotland. This incensed many people from across the social scale who were effectively being told that they must abandon Presbyterianism. Large numbers of them proclaimed, and then signed, first the National Covenant and then the Solemn League and Covenant, pledging allegiance to their original form of worship (see page 58). Unfortunately for the Covenanters, when Charles II was restored to the throne in 1660, he replaced their ally, Oliver Cromwell, and they were soon cruelly persecuted.

The period during which the persecution of Covenanters was at its height is referred to as the Killing Times. Some sources take this to refer to the 25 years spanning Charles II's reign; others date it as lasting from 1684 to 1688. Two of the most prominent persecutors were Grierson of Lag and John Graham of Claverhouse, a Highland laird and soldier of fortune, also known as Bonnie Dundee. This kenspeckle figure had returned to England after serving both the King of France and William of Orange and in 1678 was appointed troop commander in Dumfries. Much against the wishes of the townsfolk of Moffat, Claverhouse billeted his dragoons in the little town, considering it an ideal base from which to keep the surrounding area in a 'state of awe'.

The hills around Moffat provided a natural sanctuary for Claverhouse's quarry, the Covenanters. Many had to flee their homes and live like hunted animals in the nearby hills. Among them were ministers of religion, who, although obliged to abandon their churches, continued to hold religious services on the hillsides under the watchful eye of armed sentries. A couple of sites known to have been used for this purpose are the Beef Tub and Birkhill. These services came to be known as blanket preachings.

On one occasion, the militant wing of the Covenanters, the Cameronians, held a three-day conventicle up at Talla which was attended by thousands who had travelled from all over southern and mid Scotland. It was perhaps because of their numbers that Claverhouse, though he

Rough grazing land on the slopes of Upper Annandale, looking towards Hart Fell.

was reported to have been a mere four miles away, left them to get on with it. Meanwhile, further south in the Beef Tub, John Hunter scrambled desperately up the steep side of the Great Hill only to die by a musket ball fired by a dragoon – a far more typical example of Claverhouse's cruelty in hunting down the Covenanters. Claverhouse eventually met his comeuppance at Killiecrankie, when he was killed leading an unsuccessful rising of the Highland clans some years later. It is a testament to the courage and discipline of the Covenanters that in 1689 many who had fought for the cause formed the core of the new Cameronian Regiment, named after their erstwhile leader, Richard Cameron.

The Walks

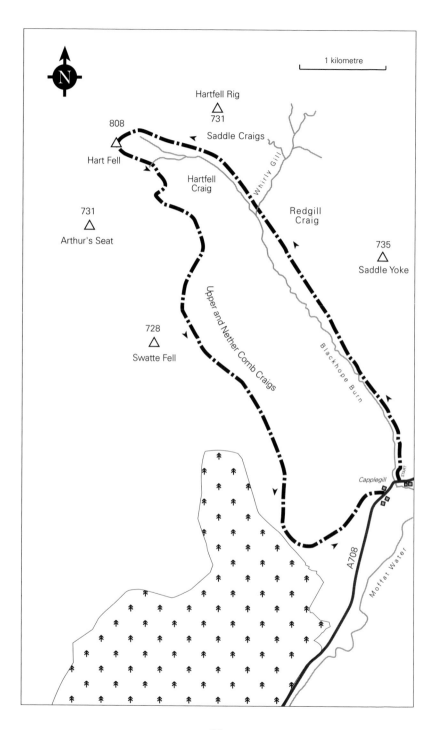

1 kilometre

N

Hartfell Rig
△
731

808
△

Saddle Craigs

Hart Fell

Hartfell
Craig

Whirly Gill

731
△
Arthur's Seat

Redgill
Craig

735
△
Saddle Yoke

Upper and Nether Comb Craigs

728
△
Swatte Fell

Blackhope Burn

Capplegill

START

A708

Moffat Water

20

When Januar' wind was blawin' cauld,
As to the North I took my way.
The mirksome night did me enfauld,
I knew na where to lodge till day.

Robert Burns, 'Adaptation of an old Cumberland Ballad'

Hart Fell and back by the Craigs

Allowing 4½ hours for this walk of 12 kilometres should give you plenty
of time to stop and admire the view, especially along the steep parts.
O.S. map 78, starting point: 147098.

There was still evidence of the recent blizzard as I parked near the
shepherd's cottage beyond Capplegill on the A708. The tops appeared
to be clear, but snow still packed the gullies. The blizzard had been
short-lived, but such was the suddenness of its onset that shepherds
counted themselves lucky to have struggled back to safety from the
hill. Less than three hundred metres from the road, nearly thirty ewes
had perished. Driven against a wire fence by the blizzard, they had
piled themselves one upon another and smothered.

The weather today was more benign. The forecast was for a hard
frost, mainly bright periods, and only the odd wintry shower. For the
dedicated hill walker or climber, it is surely the winter that brings out
the true worth of the hills.

My plans were to follow the Blackhope Burn up the glen and out
on to the plateau which would lead me to the summit of Hart Fell. The
return route, depending on the weather, would follow the ridge along
to Black Craig or involve striking north-east to Hartfell Rig and then
south-east to Saddle Yoke.

I chatted with Rab, one of Capplegill's shepherds, and advised him
of my proposed route. My spirits were high as I set off up the track with
Blackhope Burn to my left. The sky was cloudless, framed on either side
by snow-dusted crags, and the crisp, frosted grass crunched pleasantly
under my boots as I and my two dogs followed the path upwards.

As we gained height, I could see at least half a dozen ravens wheeling
round and round like black sentries, warning of an intruder entering
their remote domain. Actually that was the only wildlife we saw all
day: no sign of any mountain hares dressed in their winter coats; no

wild, frenzied cackle of grouse; no wild goats grazing the sides of the glen. Perhaps the minimal heather cover hereabouts explained the absence of grouse; the goats had probably returned to the heights after the storm.

The ridge of Saddle Yoke rose steeply to my right. This hill is perhaps one of the finest in the area, and its narrow ridge is a joy to traverse. Further up to my right the steep gully, Whirly Gill, was loaded with snow.

As we neared the point where the glen led to the summit plateau, the going got a lot steeper, and I had to kick steps in the hard, frozen snow – a pleasant task really, as it heralded the challenges to come, when the hills would assume their full winter dressing of snow. Lunch was hurriedly consumed 'cooried doon' behind the scanty shelter provided by the summit cairn on Hart Fell.

The normally fine view was obscured by a dense blanket of mist, and a freezing lazy wind probed the gaps in my shelter. So after consulting map and compass, I started off for Hartfell Craig and the ridge that would take me over Upper and Nether Coomb Craigs, with Black Hope glen down below me to the east.

I was following a compass bearing, anxious not to miss the ridge and end up on Swatte Fell or down in the wrong valley. Actually, my fears proved groundless as a fence runs along the top of the Craigs. My faithful four-legged companions had complete and misguided faith in my navigating skills and plodded on at my heel.

We had gone barely four hundred metres, when the mist suddenly lifted, and we were walking in bright winter sunshine. Believe it or not, we were smack on course, and the dogs were impressed. The ridge traverse was exhilarating as we picked our way round the Craigs. The view now was truly magnificent, with hills and glens appearing in sharp folds to the north and east.

To the far north, beyond Megget, I could see Broad Law, and to the east the Eildon Hills looked like an island floating in a sea of mist. Closer to hand, Carrifran Gans and White Coomb hovered over the road to Selkirk. (Now there's a name to conjure up all sorts of theories – Carrifran Gans. It always sounded like a Welsh name to me, but in fact 'gans' is a Scots word meaning 'jaws'.)

We gently lost height, descending from the ridge through some heather. There was a final, knee-punishing stretch as we completed the last fifty or so metres to the road.

The Megget Stone Horseshoe

This walk (9.5 km) should take just over 3 hours. O.S. maps 72, 78 and 79, starting point: 152204.

'Land of brown heath and shaggy wood/Land of mountain and the flood' – a striking description by Sir Walter Scott of the area round the Megget Stone on the small hill road between Tweedsmuir and St Mary's Loch, where one does still feel a certain sense of drama. After all, with Broad Law, Molls Cleuch Dod, Lochcraig Head and White Coomb nearby, you are surrounded by some of the highest peaks in the south of Scotland, apart from the Merrick off in the Galloway Hills.

Right up to the time of Mary, Queen of Scots, this was the area in which Scotland's nobility hunted. Vast herds of red deer, numbered in their thousands, were hunted by royalty and the aristocracy, using Cramalt Tower as their hunting lodge.

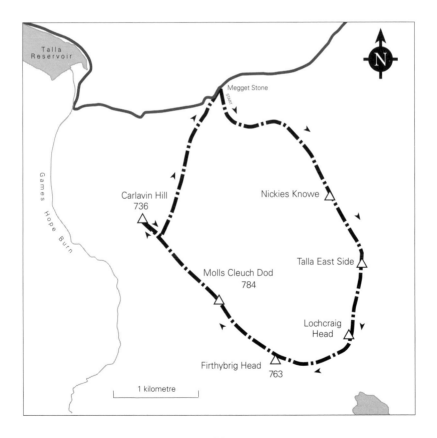

The origin of the large boulder by the roadside, known as the Megget Stone, is rather obscure. No one is sure whether it has religious or mythical significance or merely marks the boundary of the old counties of Selkirk and Peebles. Bear in mind, though, that this was the region reputedly frequented by Merlin.

As my wife and I left our car in the layby just east of the Megget Stone, snow flurries swept in from the east, borne on an icy wind; there was already a fair covering of snow as we struck off up the slopes of Wood Brae on the opposite side of the road.

At times, the snow showers blotted out our surroundings almost entirely, so we were glad to keep to the comforting fence on our right (which runs all the way to the summit of Lochcraig Head). We climbed up Nickies Knowe and Talla East Side. On a good day, it would have been the moment to pause and look back down over the reservoirs of Talla and Megget. We merely kept our heads down against the driving snow, determined not to lose sight of that fence.

Until the late seventeenth and early eighteenth centuries, all this area was part of Ettrick Forest – mixed woodland before it was cleared for sheep-farming. From Talla East Side it was an easy walk along the ridge and over the fence to the top of Lochcraig Head.

Standing on the summit, we were rewarded (between snow showers) with glimpses of Loch Skeen lying far beneath our feet, cradled dark and sparkling by the snow-covered hills surrounding it. Following the dyke westwards along the summit, we dropped down steeply to the marshy ground between Lochcraig Head and Firthybrig Head, and stopped in the shelter of the dyke to have our lunch before climbing up on to Firthybrig Head.

After lunch, we left the dyke and headed off, in the teeth of an icy wind, along the ridge to Molls Cleuch Dod. The skies cleared abruptly, and we walked the ridge in bright sunshine. It was a delight – all around, snow-clad peaks glistened in the sun. We passed the cairn on Molls Cleuch Dod and headed for the summit of Carlavin Hill. Having enjoyed the view from Carlavin, we retraced our steps and descended in a north-easterly direction over rough ground more or less parallel with Molls Cleuch Burn. We crossed the track running along the valley floor and headed back up to the road where we had parked the car.

Lowther Hill and Green Lowther

The entire walk of 12 kilometres should take a little over 3 hours. O.S. map 78, starting and finishing point: 929096.

If possible, try to choose a clear day for this walk. The views from the top of Lowther will more than recompense you for the climb up.

Leave your car in the lay-by a 100 metres north of Over Fingland farm on the A702. Part of this walk follows the Southern Upland Way.

Just south of the farm, the Upland Way takes you up by the edge of the woods and over two stiles. After the second, it follows the dyke westward through the heather to a fence. Keeping the fence to your left, go over Laght Hill, down into the bealach, up to Comb Head and Cold Moss.

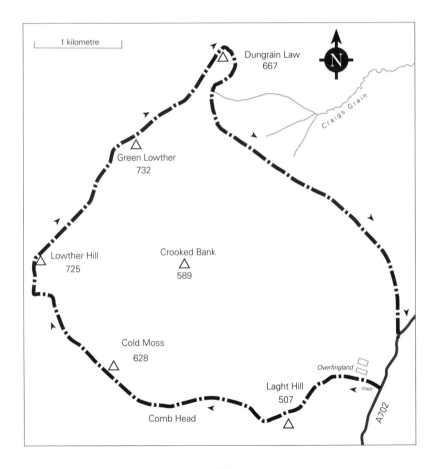

Rough going towards Lowther Hill.

Gradually the ridge (which will eventually lead right up Lowther Hill) gains height. From here the views are already breathtaking. To the west the whole Nith Valley stretches away with the hills of Galloway as a backdrop. To the south are Criffel, Screel and Bengairn by Solway's shore.

Passing the radio station, and leaving the Upland Way (which now proceeds downhill), strike north-east across the summit of Lowther Hill and head over to Green Lowther. This can usually be accomplished in about two hours.

Green Lowther also plays host to telecommunications buildings, so for solitude walk on as far as Peden Head for lunch and another splendid view. From here the Moffat Hills can easily be identified to the east; to the south-east lies Daer Reservoir. The wee village of Leadhills can be seen nestling over in the north west.

Now head for the summit of Dungrain Law. Instead of simply walking back along the centre of the ridge, skirt the vast corrie from which Craigs Grain flows. This takes you round on to the long, high, sweeping ridge of Riccart Law Rig. Follow the ridge down to the south east and back out to your car.

This is another spectacular part of the walk, because of the height of the ridge. But do look out for the numerous rabbit holes on the lower slopes. Stepping into one can result in a nasty ankle injury – as the author knows to his cost!

FEBRUARY

February fill the dyke
With what thou dost like

Thomas Tusser, from 'April's Husbandry'

White Coomb and Carrifran Circuit

This walk of 10.5 kilometres can be done in about 4 hours. O.S. map 79, starting point: 186146.

> 'Just on the edge straining his Ken,
> May view the bottom of the den,
> Where deep, deep down, and far within,
> Toils with rocks the roaring Linn,
> Then, issuing forth one foaming wave,
> And wheeling round the Giant's Grave,
> White as the snowy charger's tail,
> Drives down the pass of Moffatdale.'

So ran Sir Walter Scott's description of the Grey Mare's Tail, in *Marmion*.

Park your car in the car park next to the A708 Moffat to Selkirk road at the foot of the Grey Mare's Tail, which is well signed as a National Trust property. The famous landmark was certainly looking its best the day we started the long steep 'steg' up the path to the east of the Tail Burn and up to the hanging valley in which the remote-feeling Loch Skeen nestles like hidden treasure.

Moffat Dale is a textbook example of the effects of glaciation. Hard though it is to imagine, some millions of years ago a huge glacier stretched a distance of over forty miles from St Mary's Loch all the way to Moffat and beyond. Another glacier fed down into it from the direction of Loch Skeen. At the end of Ice Age, as it receded, it gouged out the deep cleft down which the Tail Burn plunges today. Under perfect winter conditions, these falls, which cascade some 60 metres into the chasm at their base known as the Giant's Grave, are one of the great ice climbs of Scotland.

The man-made steps that you have to climb at the beginning of the path never cease to annoy me. Laid by the National Trust to brook the process of erosion, they are so unevenly spaced that you would need to be blessed with telescopic legs to climb them comfortably. As the path gains height, threading its way up to Loch Skeen, the earth

27

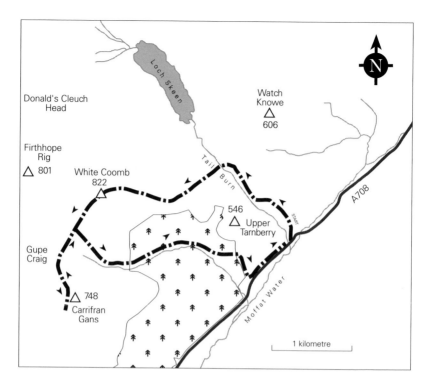

moraines left behind by the glacier are clearly visible. The path is quite steep and narrow as it contours the slopes of Bran Law. It was on these same slopes that Graham of Claverhouse, mounted on a jet-black charger, is supposed to have chased a hare and succeeded in turning it. It was muttered among the Covenanters, whom he hunted down mercilessly, that his black horse had been presented to him by the devil. Standing on the steep slopes, all I could conclude was that Auld Nick must have fitted the steed with a good set of brakes before he parted with the gift.

The first blizzards of the winter had taken their toll on the already narrow path, and parts had broken away. Anyone walking this route needs to take particular care, especially if there are children in the party. Evidence of the potential hazards can be seen if you study the rock face on the far bank. The metal rings driven into the rock are used as belay points, from which ropes can be suspended should casualties need to be brought out.

As we swung round the narrow part of the gully, the gradient eased, and we were rewarded with a fine view of the Tail Burn as it plunged into the chasm below. Above it, on the sheer cliff face, a group of feral goats, oblivious to our presence, picked a precarious route over the rocky ground. We now entered the hanging valley and, after crossing the burn, decided to follow the dyke up on to White Coomb. (The exact crossing point varies according to the depth of the water in the Tail.) Up the slope we went, with Loch Skeen lying below us to our right, bordered by Lochcraig Head at one end and Donald's Cleuch Head to its west. This beautiful wee hill loch is a favourite with fishermen, but I don't think the trout are exactly monsters. I am told, though, that larger ferox trout lurk in its depths.

On the subject of fishermen, I often wish they would they take their rubbish back down the hill with them rather than litter up the banks. It should be easier to carry empty containers, bottles and cans down the hill than it was to bring the full ones up.

The ascent became steeper as we climbed up through the heather, often disturbing red grouse, which rose with startled, cackling cries and swooped off low over the hillside. This entailed a wee bit of a scramble, before we left the dyke and headed over to the summit cairn. The cairn stands at 822 metres and it should take the average not-too-decrepit walker one and a half hours to get to it.

Weatherwise, we were now in a different world – a bitterly cold wind blew over the summit, and the grass stood frozen in petrified tufts. Time to put on another layer of clothing.

Carrifran Gans was our next objective, so we headed off to the south-west, climbing the gently ascending broad ridge, past Gupe Craig, to its summit. Still too cold for a lunch stop, so it was back to the bealach between Carrifran and White Coomb and so down the valley following the course of the burn to the south-east and keeping it to our right. At the foot of the slope was evidence of a recent avalanche in the form of large lumps of frozen snow. Lunch was taken sheltering from the icy wind beside the burn. Eventually you come out at a fence just above an old dry-stone sheep pen.

The remainder of the walk is a pleasant contrast to the hill, as you gently lose height, following a grassy track through the forest. Just ahead of us a roe deer, startled by our approach, glided effortlessly away into the trees; we also spotted some owl pellets. Follow the wide forestry ride heading off to the south east until it peters out. Then carry on through the trees until you emerge on the eastern edge of the plantation. Follow the fence steeply down this edge to the road. A short walk will bring you back to the car.

A word of warning: in summer, the area after the forest track comes to an end becomes very overgrown with bracken, so this is definitely a walk to keep for the spring or autumn.

The Captain's Road

This 20-kilometre walk takes about 5½ hours. O.S. maps 79, 73, starting and finishing point: 241205.

Tibbie Shiels, a couthie snug wee place, nestles between the Loch of the Lowes and St Mary's Loch at the head of the Yarrow Valley; it lies equidistant between Moffat and Selkirk just off the A708. The longest serving host at the inn (which was originally known as St Margaret's Cottage) was a Mrs Richardson. She must have spent her whole life there, for she was resident for ninety-seven years. It is thought that her maiden name was Shiels, making her in all probability the original Tibbie.

Just over the main road from the hotel, the statue of James Hogg, the Ettrick Shepherd, gazes out over the valley and his favourite and well-kent hills (he worked as a shepherd in Yarrow for nine years). Hector, his much-loved sheep dog, lies at his master's feet. The haunting last line from the Queen's Wake, inscribed on the plinth, seems an apt tribute to the Border poet: 'He taught the wandering winds to sing'.

Leaving the car near Tibbie Shiels Inn, my wife and I set off east along the track pressing uphill past Crosscleuch farm. Look out for the Southern Upland Way sign, then turn right along the Way for a short distance (making a small detour on to Earl's Hill if you fancy the view), then head down through a conifer plantation. Not far along, another sign points up to the left to meet the so-called 'Captain's Road'. I've never found out just who the Captain was. Maybe he was some drouthy gent over in Ettrick who journeyed back and forth to Tibbie Shiels Inn to quench his thirst.

The Captain's Road is well surfaced here, as it emerges from the trees before heading down into Ettrick. However, we did find the going a bit messy as we tried to cross Hopehouse Burn so that we could walk the length of the valley.

Having passed through Thirlstanehope farm, we joined the main road (B709) at Wardlaw and headed south-west towards the wee village of Ettrick. This is perhaps the worst part of the walk: the tarmac seems awful hard after walking on the hill. In Ettrick, turn right on to the minor road to Scabcleuch, passing on your way the monument on the birthplace of James Hogg.

Actually you can turn off to the right early at Ettrick Church and then follow the left bank of the burn behind the church (which we did because we were fed up with the tarmac). This leads you up round the edge of Craig Hill to link up with the Upland Way beneath Peniestone Knowe. We took this short cut, but were not rewarded because it turned out to be wet and boggy and the path rather indistinct.

It's probably better to go a bit further to Scabcleuch, where you turn right up the Upland Way as it skirts the slopes of Peniestone Knowe and follow the sweep of the valley round before climbing up over Pikestone Rig. This part of the route is an absolute joy. You go the length of a most attractive valley, and the surface of the path makes for easy walking.

By the time we reached the valley, the temperature had dropped again, but after the steamy walk round the road and the squelch out to join the Way, the lazy chill wind was almost welcome.

To the left, before you climb up over Pikestone Rig, there's a path leading off down to the shores of the Loch of the Lowes which you can

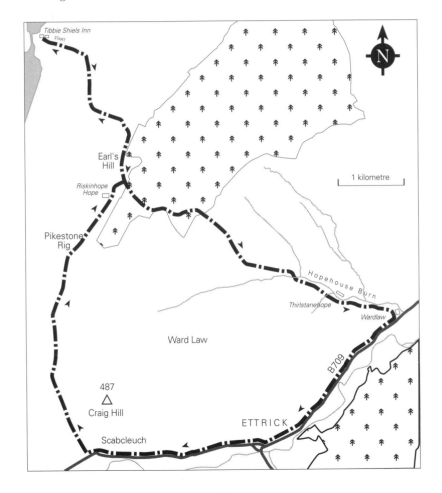

follow round to Tibbie Shiels. However, I think it's better to stay with the Way as it crosses the high ground before dropping down to the bridge at Riskinhope Hope. The scenery along this section of the Way must be among the best.

Crossing the bridge, we climbed back up to rejoin the original outward route. About now, Mother Nature, deciding to have the last word, drenched us with an icy wintry shower before we could reach the car.

The Ettrick Shepherd watches over St Mary's Loch.

When that Aprille with his shoures sote
The droghte of Marche perced to the rote.

Geoffrey Chaucer, *Canterbury Tales*

The Bodesbeck Ridge

The time for the 19-kilometre round trip, returning by road, is 6 hours.
O.S. maps 78 and 79, starting point: 147098.

The forecast was for a cold clear day – surely good for ridge-walking.
But as my wife and I drove up Moffat Water to park the car just beyond
Capplegill, the valley floor was enveloped in thick mist. Then we met
Tom Murray, the head shepherd at Capplegill, who assured us that the
tops would be clear, and cheered up.

Our intention was to climb on to Bodesbeck Law and walk the ridge,
heading north-east, then to descend off Herman Law at Birkhill. It
always seems to me that this ridge neatly divides the Moffat Hills from
Ettrick to the east. It is fairly high (at no point does it drop below 550
metres) – and on a clear day the views are first-class.

It's perhaps advisable to have the use of two cars for this walk, or to
have a driver prepared to pick you up at the far end. The alternative
is to retrace your steps along the ridge or to walk back along the road.

We crossed the road and followed the track up to Bodesbeck farm,
turning left at the top of the hill and heading down towards the steading. There we took the gateway on the right following the track over a
branch of Bodesbeck Burn. As we steadily gained height, the winding
path remained shrouded by mist. We must have been at 300 metres
when we suddenly found ourselves in bright sunshine.

Here was a perfect example of temperature inversion. Below us
Moffat Water was a sea of white, swirling mist, stretching away to the
edge of Annandale, while we were bathed in bright sunshine.

The winter grasses on the nearby slopes of White Shank assumed a
soft, ochre glow as they were brushed by the morning sun. On the
opposite side of the valley, Saddle Yoke and Carrifran Gans rose steeply
from the mist with the snow-dusted crest of White Coomb peeping out
behind. It was a view to savour.

As we gazed down, the first of three low-flying jet aircraft shot past.
It seemed to round the corner out of Annandale and, followed by its

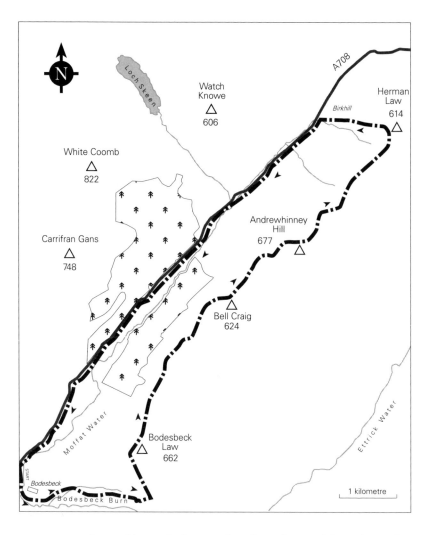

two companions, skimmed along at break-neck speed just above the white sea of cloud in the valley beneath our feet.

The path leads on down into Ettrick and on to the bothy at Phawhope, but we left it here where it is dissected by the county boundary fence, and followed the fence uphill to the summit of Bodesbeck Law.

Tales of the famous Brownie of Bodesbeck, reported to have frequented this area in the mid seventeenth century, have their origins in both fact and myth. There are various, often confusing, accounts. At that time, the inhabitants of Moffat Water and other remote valleys were extremely superstitious, believing that the surrounding hills were occupied by brownies, fairies and evil creatures. They even believed that a harmless wild animal like the mountain hare could turn into a supernatural creature by night.

Their imaginings of strange goings-on were further encouraged by sightings of mysteriously flashing lights at dead of night and the sound of unexplained bird calls. For those same hills were a refuge for hundreds of Covenanters, who could move and communicate only under cover of darkness. These were indeed the Killing Times when the Covenanters were ruthlessly persecuted by Claverhouse and Grierson of Lag and their Dragoons.

According to James Hogg, the Ettrick Shepherd, some of the Covenanters were given succour by a certain Walter Laidlaw of Chapelhope up in Yarrow. Hogg and other sources refer to the Brownie of Bodesbeck haunting 'Wattie's' house in the form of a dragon.

Others say that the Brownie was in fact a Cameronian who sheltered in a cave on Bodesbeck. He was given food by Walter and his daughter and repaid them by doing their field work at night, returning to his cave before daybreak. This cave was seemingly covered up years later by a landslip.

Sir Walter Scott also contributed his pennyworth, claiming that there was a real Brownie living on Bodesbeck – the last one known in Ettrick Forest. An old lady left out some milk and money in payment for favours received. But it seems to have been the worst thing she could have done: he left the area the following day. So who do you believe?

No Brownies or Covenanters about today, so we followed the ridge along over Bell Craig and on to the top of Andrewhinney Hill. From here we looked over the valley and into the heart of the Moffat Hills. You get a first-class view from here of the Grey Mare's Tail and the path leading up to Loch Skeen.

Incidentally, if you happen to be walking the ridge in the mist, you will never go wrong if you follow the fence, remembering that it heads off west as it comes down off Herman Law at the end.

After a fairly steep stomp down off Herman Law we picked up the road at Birkhill Cottage. The walk back to Capplegill, which we did, is long and tedious, so I advise you to organise some transport.

Carrifran Glen and Carrifran.
Looking across from Bodesbeck into the Moffat Hills.

Over into Ettrick

The time for this 13.5 kilometre walk is just over 4 hours. O.S. map 79, starting point: 147098.

Drive up the A708 from Moffat and leave the car near Blackshope cottage. Walk up the loaning that leads over the bridge spanning Moffat Water towards Bodesbeck farm. After passing through the gateway above the steading, cross a branch of Bodesbeck Burn. The footpath then leads uphill, with White Shank over to the right and Bodesbeck Law at the end of the ridge to the left.

The path climbs gently for about two kilometres, and is crossed by the fence that marks the old country boundaries between Dumfriesshire and Selkirkshire. The fence leads up to the summit of Bodesbeck Law (once the home of the celebrated Brownie), but our route wends its way between two forest plantations and emerges near the small farm of Potburn in the Ettrick Valley.

Make your way around the outside of the farm, and join the Upland Way, following it southwards towards the head of the valley. Eventually,

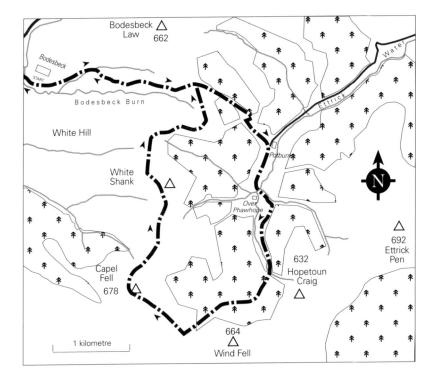

you arrive at the bridge at Over Phawhope, and on the other side of the bridge is Phawhope bothy. Owned by the Scottish Mountain Bothy Association, Phawhope is maintained by volunteers. Most bothies lie in remote areas, so raise your hat to the dedicated souls who carry in all the materials for their upkeep. It's a great pity that some of the bothies' tenants don't show the same dedication in their respect for the facilities. Being on the Way, Phawhope is a popular howf with the distance walkers.

It was a cold day when my wife and I did the walk, so we were glad to eat our lunch sitting inside. We were joined by a lone walker who happened to be doing our route in reverse. It was fine to have a chat with a kindred spirit before leaving to take the track uphill through the forest.

After some time, we cleared the forest at Ettrick Head. Here the Upland Way Path becomes narrower, and shortly afterwards it is crossed by the boundary fence. At the fence (rather than after it), climb steeply to the right up the slopes of Capel Fell; where the fence gives way to a well-maintained dyke, carry on along the ridge to White Shank, where fine views down Ettrick Valley and over into Annandale open up before you.

Follow the dyke along the ridge, ignoring the fence going off to the right (otherwise you'll end up back down in Ettrick Valley). Eventually the dyke becomes dilapidated but is replaced by a fence, with which you keep company, heading first east, then north back to the gate you originally came through.

Coming back down to Bodesbeck there are some splendid views across the valley to Black Hope glen, Saddle Yoke, White Coomb and Carrifran.

Wedder Law

This walk of 10 kilometres should take about 3½ hours. O.S. map 78, starting point: 962054.

Turning off the A702, follow the sign for Daer Reservoir and drive round its west shore. There is a parking place, just off the track, about four hundred metres beyond Kirkhope farm.

This route leads you up Wedder Law and back following the ridge round to come full circle. Cross the bridge over Carsehope Burn, then follow the track, which hugs the banks of Daer Water, and proceed up to the head of the valley. As I started this walk, I mused about the origin of the hill's name. A wedder, or wether, is a castrated sheep

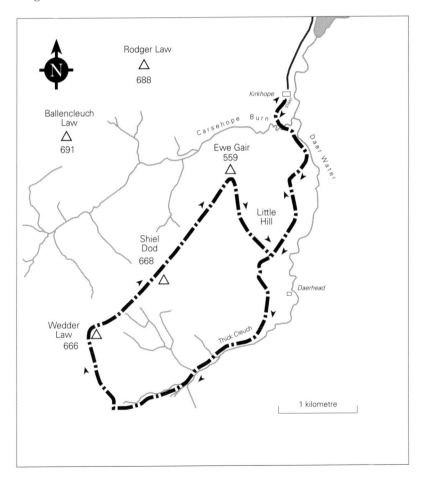

which is fattened for slaughter. Perhaps all the wethers were kept on this hill before being sent to market.

Ignore the track that takes off to the left to the now-deserted steading at Daerhead. Shortly afterwards, the vehicle track ends; follow a rather indistinct path uphill that heads south-west into open country between two gateposts (no fence attached). Thick Cleuch burn on your left wends its way in a rather discreet fashion over the heather-clad hags towards the fence that runs off Five Wells and up the slopes of Wedder Law, marking the old county boundary between Dumfries-shire and Lanarkshire. When you reach the fence, turn right (to the north) and follow the fence up to the summit of Wedder Law.

We were astounded at the number of mountain hares, still sporting their white winter coats, sitting on the slopes of the hill and apparently untroubled by our presence. The views from the summit were first-class.

The path going north-east along the ridge towards Shiel Dod is well defined and joins up with the stalkers' vehicle track. I noticed by the map that Shiel Dod is a mere two metres higher than Wedder Law.

From Shiel Dod you have a choice of two routes back to the car. Either take the vehicle track as it twists its way back to where the paths separated near the two gateposts; you would then follow the path east back towards the car. Or you can do as we did, and keep to the ridge as far as Ewe Gair before descending to the valley floor by following the wee burn to the south-east of the summit.

The Black Esk

About 12 kilometres. With a stop for lunch, and allowing time to admire the pools at Garwaldshiels, the walk should take approximately 3 hours. O.S. map 79, starting and finishing point: 208938.

This is a low-level walk, out through one of Eskdale's largest forests, just to the south of Moffatdale. When my wife and I walked it, the weather was frosty and clear, but it would also make an ideal walk for a day when the conditions were not quite right for going on to the tops.

The starting point for this walk is about 7 kilometres east of the village of Boreland on the B723 to Eskdalemuir. Your car can be parked just off the road, half a kilometre east of Sandyford, at the entrance to the forest track on the lefthand side of the road. Don't be confused by the large area of trees in Castle O'er Forest as shown on the map: large parts of it have either been cleared or felled and recently re-planted, so the trees are still very young, and thus not tall enough to obscure the good views all round. It's encouraging to see how many deciduous trees have been planted this time round.

Over to the east lies the small hamlet of Twiglees. Twiglees appeared on Blaeu's map of 1660, which gives the meaning of the name as a clearing in the forest. Apparently the whole parish of Eskdalemuir – the largest in old Dumfriesshire – was, like nearby Ettrick Forest itself, covered in ancient forest. By the eighteenth century the valley had been cleared of trees to make way for large numbers of sheep. Events have now come full circle, and today Eskdalemuir is one of the most afforested parishes in Scotland, with Twiglees being one of the first forests to be planted in the 1900s. Most of the planting you can now see dates from the 1960s. Quite near Twiglees lies the site of one of the many Roman forts and settlements in this area, established between 80 AD and 180 AD to protect the numerous roads that passed through the valley.

Head north into the plantation; a hundred yards along, ignore the track going off to the left and keep heading north-east. It's quite open here and we had a fine view of the snow-covered peaks of Ettrick Pen and Hopetoun Craig lying away to the north behind a chequered winter landscape of browns and dark greens. Soon we were surrounded by mature Sitka spruce – the track now covered in frozen snow. Out into the open again, and we looked to our left over recently planted ground. Up on a mature tree on the other side of the road was nailed an old oil drum. This is an area inhabited by the short-eared owl, and sometimes the old owl is given a wee bit of a hand with the housing.

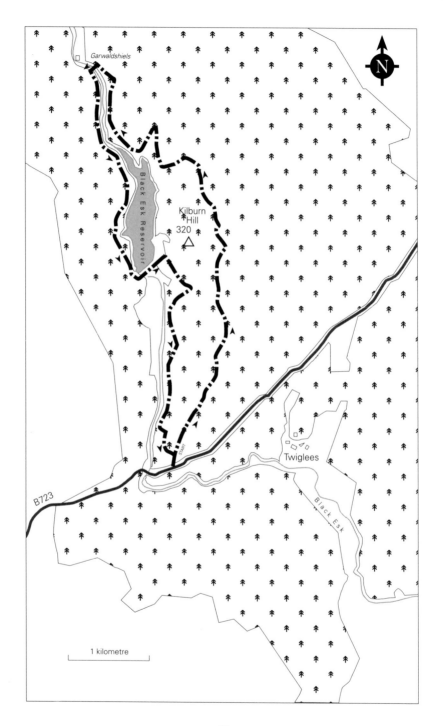

Garwaldshiels

Black Esk Reservoir

Kilburn
Hill
320

START

Twiglees

B723

Black Esk

N

1 kilometre

Seemingly its main source of food is the short-tailed vole. No sign of owls today, but the bobbing white tails of two large roe deer appeared momentarily as they glided effortlessly up the hill through the trees.

Away back at the end of the eighteenth century, the population of the parish was 619, and it's interesting to know how their material needs were catered for. There were three merchants, a miller, three wrights, two blacksmiths, four tailors, a clogger and nine weavers. Winters in those days must have been a lot worse – especially in 1794, when over four thousand sheep were lost in a snowstorm, and more went down the burn when the thaw came in the spring.

At the point where a small sign says 'Rashieknowe', we dropped down to join the track which circumnavigates the Black Esk reservoir. Turning right here, we walked once more through mature trees, crossed over the Whirl Burn, and turned left towards the reservoir, picking up a musk-like scent indicating that a fox had recently crossed our path. Over in the ditch beside the track were early signs that spring might not be far off: the first frogspawn of the year among fresh watercress. Soon the path took us round to the pools where the Esk gushes under the bridge at Garwaldshiels on its way towards the reservoir. The chance of a swim was too great for the two dogs to resist, and I marvelled at their courage, swimming in that ice-cold water.

At this point you turn south and walk along the track skirting the west bank of the reservoir. Stop and have a look at the numerous bird boxes put up by schoolchildren along the way. Among them can be seen bat boxes with their opening at the bottom as well as more owl drums. The Black Esk reservoir has a catchment of nearly five thousand acres and when it was opened in 1962, it added 500 million gallons to the region's water resources, with a daily output of seven million gallons. It took nearly ten years to complete the scheme; more than five metres' depth of glacial deposits lies at its bottom and stops the water seeping away.

After passing the boat house at the southern end of the reservoir, we climbed over the gate and walked over the top of the dam, then went uphill to join the path to the east. Turn right here and follow the path out towards the starting point. It traverses the slopes of Kilburn Hill and offers fine views of the valley below.

O! how the spring of love resembleth,
The uncertain glory of an April day.

William Shakespeare, *Two Gentlemen of Verona*

Hartfell Spa and Hart Fell

5 hours for this 13-kilometre walk. O.S. maps 78 and 79, starting point:
075104.

One of the greatest pleasures in life is to renew an old acquaintance.
One April weekend I decided to do just that and return to a favourite
walk of mine. I parked the car 3 kilometres or so outside Moffat at the
Annan Water Hall on the Old Edinburgh Road, a continuation of
Beechgrove (into which you turn right off the A701 as it leaves the
town and passes Moffat Academy). This road eventually ends at the
bottom of the Beef Tub. Unfortunately, the weather man was not
smiling on this meeting of old friends, and the rain came on as soon
as I left the car.

The route follows the signs to Hartfell Spa with, over on the right,
the Auchencat Burn gushing its way to meet the infant Annan. Two

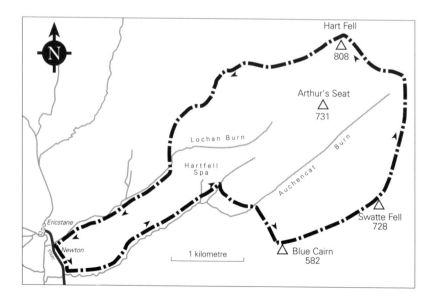

Hart Fell.

oystercatchers kept a wary eye from the burnside, but there was no sign of the heron which frequently fishes here – perhaps the angling season had yet to begin. After the high ground, the path plunges down to meet the burn which is crossed, and then recrossed, by two wooden bridges.

The valley sides are a lot steeper by this point, and the rain was getting heavier as we followed the rough path skirting the burn. About 2 kilometres from the road, the path veers off to the left into the deep cleft gouged into the base of Arthur's Seat. This leads to Hartfell Spa, which is worth a visit.

The three springs in the vicinity of Moffat – Moffat Well at Archbank, Garpol Spa and Hartfell Spa certainly put the wee town on the map as a favourite tourist spot, and thus assured the future of the honest citizens of the burgh. Archbank and Garpol were discovered way back in the first half of the seventeenth century. However, Hartfell Spa was discovered by a farmer some hundred years later. John Williamson was supervising a mining operation further down the burn when he made his discovery. The spring issues from a vaulted structure made of brick and set into the black shale of the hillside.

It was in the mid-nineteenth century that real prosperity was brought to the town when a number of Edinburgh physicians made some impressive claims for the healing qualities of the spa waters. Those who imbibed the waters, it was said, would gain relief from such ailments as gravel, diseases of the skin, rheumatism, biliousness and even infections of the lung. The daily dose of this supposed panacea was a mind-boggling pint – yugh!

The Ordnance Survey gazetteer for 1864 states: 'The water is a powerful tonic, cool, and acidious, specially good for dyspepsia'. Some writers were more honest and described the taste as 'Resembling bilgewater or the scourings from a foul gun'; another: 'It has the taste and smell of slightly putrescent egg.'

I retraced my steps to cross the burn and start up the steep heatherclad slopes of Blue Cairn. This is really quite a hard slog, but the gradient eases as you follow the path up to the summit of Swatte Fell. By now the weather had completely closed in and we were enveloped in a dense blanket of mist.

My advice, if you arrive here in such conditions, is to follow the fence, keeping it on your right. My intention was to cross over Swatte Fell then climb up over Hartfell Craig on to Hart Fell.

The summit cairn of Swatte Fell loomed eerily out of the mist as I passed, always aware of the comforting presence of the fence on my right. As long as I followed this fence and ignored the three that join it,

I knew I would eventually end up at the trig point on Hart Fell.

By the time I arrived there the weather was pretty foul – cold, driving rain and a thick mist – so lunch was eaten hurriedly in a crouched position behind the scanty shelter provided by the trig point. There was only one four-legged companion to share my lunch today, as her pal was indisposed – no place to bring a (hopefully) pregnant mum.

My plan was to return to the Annan Valley by following the Pot and Lochan Burns as they descend the valley out to Newton farm. So it was time to sever myself from the reassurance of the fence, take a compass bearing, and strike out over the shoulder of Hart Fell to the south-west.

I could feel the slope getting steeper as I followed my bearing when, as so often happens in the hills, the mist just rolled away. Below me lay the Pot Burn.

The descent through the wild valley is really worthwhile. There are no distinct paths to follow, as it's a route not often taken, and you cross and recross the burn frequently. The burn, which is punctuated by pools often shaded by the occasional birch or rowan, is a delight to walk along. In the summer I've bathed in its pools; a bit too cold for that today.

Just after it is crossed by a footbridge, the Lochan plunges through a series of gullies thickly clad with birch, larch and evergreens, and you come upon a path that follows the contours of the slopes and eventually takes you to the sheep pens at Newton. It's only a short walk from here to the car. Feeling slightly damp, I peeled off my waterproofs, but it had been a great day.

After all, if you can't accept that every day in the hills may not be sunny, maybe it's time to take up the bingo.

Queensberry

Allow 4 hours for this walk of 11.5 kilometres. O.S. map 78, starting and finishing point: 034016.

Queensberry, the hill that rises up between Nithsdale and Annandale, can be climbed from either valley. If you approach it from Nithsdale, Mitchellslacks is a suitable starting point. As a resident of Annandale, I prefer to ascend from the Beattock side. Queensberry appears to sit on its own, a landmark visible from afar, and an outrider of the Lowthers looking over the Annandale plain towards the Moffat Hills in the east. It's a pretty uninteresting hill itself, but affords superb views all round.

I take the Crooked Road (or Windy Brae, as it is known locally) which starts opposite Beattock House Hotel in the village and winds up towards Kinnelhead farm. Normally I park the car, after passing Easter and Wester Earshaig, just before the bridge spanning Kinnel Water.

Beyond the shepherd's cottage on the left, we take the track to the left, heading south-west towards Lochanhead cottage. Short of the cottage, cross over the rough ground and head towards the edge of Ae Forest – one of the largest conifer plantations in Britain.

Follow the forestry fence in a westerly direction up to the metal gate just below Queensberry summit. On my first visit here, I was surprised by how rocky it is; a huge pile of stones serves as its cairn. The views from the summit are unsurpassed. Over to the west lies Nithsdale and to the south the Lake District hills provide a backdrop to the Solway tides. Over to the east you can make out the mass of the Cheviots.

Keeping to the high ground, the return route goes via Mount Glass and Harestanes Heights with its distinctive cairn. From there, follow the ridge eastwards over Peat Hill and descend by the path to Lochanhead.

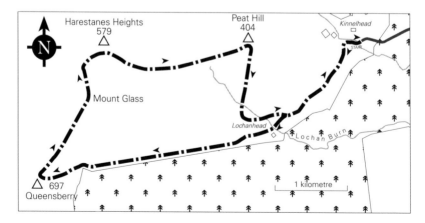

The Caledonian Railway

This walk, if the weather obliges, must rate as one of the finest low-level walks in south-west Scotland, and April is probably the optimum time to do it. The distance is 10 kilometres and it should take about 2¼ hours. We enjoyed the walk so much that we took a return on the old railway and then walked back in the other direction. O.S. map 78, starting and finishing point: 955168.

At the end of the last century, passengers waiting to board the little train that ran from Elvanfoot out along the Elvan valley to Wanlockhead would apparently slake their thirst at the local inn before proceeding to the railway station. This line, which was run by the Caledonian Railway Company, served not just to transport minerals from the mines, but provided their main contact with the outside world for the inhabitants of Scotland's highest village. This must surely have been one of the most scenic railway journeys in Scotland, as the train snaked its way through the hills around the village.

The station and the inn at Elvanfoot are long since gone, as is the railway itself, which disappeared even before Dr Beeching began his dastardly assaults on local lines. But I decided to walk the track from Elvanfoot up to Wanlockhead in an attempt to recapture just what it must have been like to make the journey by train.

A car can be parked near the little church in Elvanfoot, on the A702. Walk north along the road and follow the track which leads up to the electricity sub-station, which you round on its north side. Immediately afterwards, you pick up the old railway track. The old railway ballast is now well covered over with grass, making for a good walking surface. It's quite open here, and a lazy wind made sure we kept up a good pace, though the sun shone and visibility was perfect. You do need a clear day for this walk to appreciate the views; on a misty wet day, most of its charm would be hidden.

The old railway track leads in a great sweep round to the north, over the open moor, as it heads (towards Leadhills) to the Elvanfoot road, out through a cutting and over a bridge high over Elvan Water. After the bridge, follow the track up to the road which it crosses before it heads west across the hillside. I wondered if there might once have been some kind of level crossing here. Perhaps not, as I don't suppose the road was too busy in those days; it's not exactly a bustling highway today either.

As we climbed up behind North Shortcleugh farm, I could just imagine the children there running out to greet the wee train, its

piercing whistle proclaiming its arrival as it puffed noisily above the house and on up the valley. Perhaps it stopped sometimes to pick up the farmer's wife on her way to Wanlockhead or Leadhills for her shopping. If she made the journey during August, the heather-clad hills would have been in full bloom and, with the train climbing ever higher along the flank of the valley, she would have seen to the south the big humps of Dun Law, Green Lowther and finally Lowther Hill itself standing stark and steep.

The bulk of the traffic on this line, however, was freight from the numerous lead and silver mines dotted around the hills. We were now

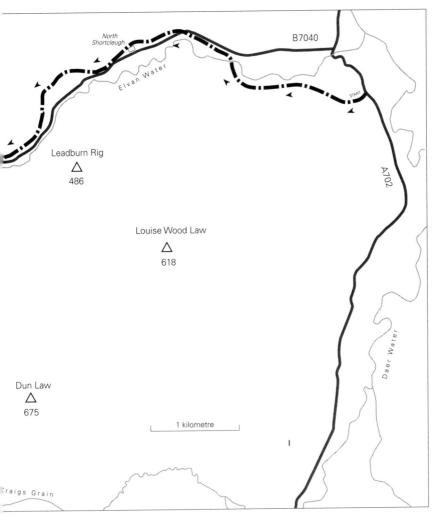

approaching the first of them as we broached the gentle incline, the track cutting across the flanks of Wellgrain Dod, with the road and Elvan Water below us. There are signs of workings to the left, and further on you come upon still more to the right. You can still make out the small spoil heaps and evidence of vertical shafts and adits. This area and further out on Crawford Muir were the areas where gold was found.

Gold was discovered in these parts during the reign of James IV, and it is said that at the wedding feast in 1542 for his son and Madeline of France, the goblets filled with gold that were placed on the tables, and the King's and Queen's crowns, incorporated gold mined from this

The Mennock Pass near Wanlockhead.
Panning for gold in Elvan Water.

area. These crowns were no lightweights at 35 ounces and 46 ounces respectively. Apparently the annual revenue at this time from the gold mines in the area amounted to £100,000 – a not inconsiderable sum in those days.

However, it was lead and, to a lesser degree, silver, that were later to provide the reasons for most of the freight traffic on the wee railway. As late as 1885, the average annual output of mines in the area was 1,000 tons of lead and 5,750 ounces of silver.

Soon you reach a gully that was once straddled by a huge viaduct, which, alas, is no more. So we had to scramble down to the burn (Shortcleugh Water) and up the other side of the valley. Shortly after this, you have to join the main road that has climbed steeply from below to intersect with the track on the outskirts of Leadhills. You cross over it and then pick up the track again, where, at one time, a railway bridge crossed the road. The path takes you along the side of a golf course, which must surely be the highest in Scotland. The day we were there, one hardy soul was braving the elements and striking a fair ball into the bargain. We soon arrived at Leadhills railway station, which still has its railway lines and some of the original rolling stock. For this is the home of the Leadhills and Wanlockhead Railway, a group of railway enthusiasts who are relaying the track between the two villages. With its fully restored platform and sidings, it is really quite impressive.

Pushing on towards Wanlockhead, we followed the newly laid track for about half a mile and wished the society luck with the laying of the remainder. Mine Hill was on our left as we walked parallel to the main road. The hill is aptly named – its flanks are a mass of old mine workings, some of which were obviously quite extensive.

We soon arrived in Wanlockhead, a village whose entire population would at one time have been engaged in clawing out the valuable metals that lay underground. Religion was obviously high on the list of priorities, for in 1755 a church was built that would accomodate over three hundred souls. It cost the princely sum of seventy pounds. In 1848, the Duke of Buccleuch built the villagers a replacement which held over four hundred. The Free Kirk followers had to wait a bit longer (eleven years to be exact) before they got a place in which to worship. Until then their ministers held services on the open hillsides. With the Covenanting history of this area this was no innovation – just a re-run of the blanket preachings of the Killing Times.

Rough winds do shake the darling buds of May,
And summer's lease hath all too short a date.

William Shakespeare, *Sonnet XVIII*

The Loch Skeen Circuit

Allow yourself 4 hours for this 12-kilometre walk so that you have plenty
of time to savour the views. O.S. map 79, starting point ref: 186146.

A chill wind greeted us as we left the car in the car park on the A708 at
the foot of the Grey Mare's Tail. However, the cloud was high, most of
the tops were visible, and the forecast had promised us better things
as the day progressed.

Our intention was to do the Loch Skeen Circuit. This is a round of
the tops that cradle the loch, which allows you to keep the water within
sight for most of the walk. The trip is really only advisable on a clear
day if you are to savour its delights to the full. We took the high path

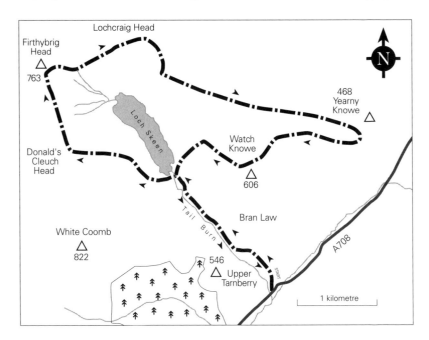

which runs along the flanks of Bran Law, and climbed steeply up towards Loch Skeen.

The sun broke through as we crossed the Tail Burn, where it spills out of Loch Skeen, and picked our way over the rough ground approaching the base of Donald's Cleuch Head. Here you take a clearly defined path which gently twists its way, alpine style, up the steep end of the ridge.

The Moffat Hills are not liberally endowed with paths, perhaps no bad thing really. But this hill is an exception, and a path follows its entire length. You get a much better view, though, if you stray from the path to the edge of the ridge which rises steeply from the shores of the loch. When we were there, a bitter May wind cut at us and sent ripples racing over the surface of the water far below. The colour of the loch changed frequently as, chameleon-like, it reflected the rapidly altering moods of the sky. This lofty perch is a fine place to pause, cushioned by the springy heather and cloudberry bushes, deciding that you're not in a hurry anyway.

At the outset of the climb up the zig-zag path on to the ridge is an area of special interest to the botanist. Over to the south-west is another hanging valley nestling in the skirts of White Coomb, which is rich in alpine plants and well worth a visit. However, as the Bard said, 'Pleasures are like poppies spread...', so we had, reluctantly, to leave our perch on the summit of Donald's Cleuch and follow the ridge along to Firthybrig Head. Here you keep company with the dyke as it drops down into the hollow, and then start the long, steep plod up to Lochcraig Head. As you get your head down to tackle the climb, it's worth glancing over your shoulder to the north, where Broadlaw, with its radio dome, peeps over the tops of two nearer hills rejoicing in the couthie names of Molls Cleuch Dod and Nickies Knowe. You wonder at this stage how all the hills in this area got their names. Were they perhaps named after local shepherds?

Such trivia can keep your mind off the hard slog up to the summit. However, we were soon there, and rewarded by a different view of the loch, this time looking straight down its length. We crossed the summit, picked up the dyke again and followed it down off the hill, knees protesting at the sharp descent. Lunch was taken in the biel of the dyke, sheltering from the ever-present, bitter wind.

The dyke marks both the National Trust and old county boundaries. It was now time to change direction. Our intention was to cross the broken ground and end up above Birkhill cottage on the Selkirk road. To achieve this, it's a good idea to set off in the direction of Herman Law on the Ettrick Side of the valley. Now there's a queer name for you. Could there have been a German shepherd loose in the hills at some time?

We crossed some pretty rough territory on this part of the walk, spending a lot of time picking our way through the peat hags in an easterly direction as far as Yearny Knowe. As we clambered higher, we looked back at the formation of the hills where we had just been. If it had been in the Pyrenees, someone would have identified it as a *cirque*. Below us, but out of sight, lay Birkhill cottage, just where the road climbs steeply out of the head of Moffat Dale and freewheels down into Yarrow.

There's a lot of history to this lonely wee dwelling. A plaque on the wall tells us that Charles Lapworth worked around here, dating various rock stata. He was a schoolmaster from Galashiels who spent much of his time on the shale-covered hillsides nearby. Graptolites – the fossils of extinct sea creatures from the Silurian period, 440-480 million years ago – were his forte. Lapworth's efforts were eventually rewarded when he was made the first Professor of Geology at Birmingham University.

Far more interesting is Birkhill's history as a cottage inn used right up to the late nineteenth century by travellers. The area was much frequented by Covenanters. The hill opposite was used as a look-out point during blanket preachings, hence its name, Watch Knowe. The arch villain of the Killing Times, Bonnie Dundee, shot two young Covenanters who were brothers in cold blood right on the doorstep of the cottage.

About that time, further down the valley into Moffat Dale, two characters named Halbert Dobson and David Dun, known as Hab Dob and Davie Din, lived in a dwelling built on the edge of a cliff for safety. Today the rather forbidding burn and gully are named Dob's Lin.

In more peaceful times, perhaps the most celebrated hostess here was Jenny, the herd's wife, who entertained Sir Walter Scott on his way to and from Drumlanrig Castle. Jenny may even have comforted him after both he and his horse got submerged in the mire near the Tail.

On leaving Yearny Knowe, head west until you pick up the National Trust fence again, and follow it up over the top of Watch Knowe, then proceed gently downhill and join the path just below the loch. Having reached this point, we took a last look at the loch and surrounding hills bathed in late afternoon sunshine, then went back down the path to the car.

The Grey Mare's Tail from Bran Law.

High Abune Sanquhar

Allow 3 hours for this 10-kilometre walk. O.S. map 78, starting and finishing point: 801116.

'Abune', for those not familiar with the Scots tongue, means above; Robert Burns used it to describe the culinary prowess of the haggis:

> 'Fair fa' your honest sonsie face,
> Great chieftain o' the puddin-race.
> Aboon them a' ye tak your place . . .'

Sanquhar was until the 1960s a thriving coal-mining community; back in the seventeenth century it had also been a hotbed of Covenanter sympathies. It was here, on 22nd June 1680, that Richard Cameron pinned up on the market cross the Sanquhar Declaration denouncing the religion of the Establishment. Later the same year, he was hunted down and killed by the dragoons for his trouble. But the Covenanters were a determined lot, and five years later one James Renwick pinned up another document: the Sanquhar Protestation. He proved harder to lay hands on, and it was three years before the dragoons caught and hanged him.

The starting point for this walk requires careful seeking out. From the main street in Sanquhar, heading north, turn up St Mary's Street opposite an outfitter's shop just before the tollbooth. Follow this narrow street over the railway bridge and all the way up into the hills, until you reach a small road leading to Clenries farm on your left and Auchentaggart Moor to your right. You can park your car close to the ruined cottage.

Walk up the road that heads up to the farm, passing a small reservoir on your right. The tarmac comes to an end, and the track continues towards the small steading of Mossholm. From here there are fine views of Crawick Water down to the left as you skirt Conrig Hill. The path now crosses the slopes of Fingland Rig. (Ignore the track swinging down to the left and back towards Knockenhair.) Once on the open hillside, the path drops down towards Nether Cog and the bridge over Crawick Water.

Our route leads off up to the right, through a gateway and along the edge of the forest. The monotony of the conifer plantation is pleasantly relieved by the presence of some fine silver birches and rowans. This rather delightful path meanders uphill and down, in and out of the trees, before finally dropping down sharply and then climbing again towards the ruined farmhouse of Cogshead. After the path emerges from the trees, there is a stile on the right, which leads on to the Southern Upland Way.

Following the marker posts, climb over the hill heading west. Once on the plateau, it is worth pausing for a moment to admire the view of Upper Nithsdale. You may be lucky enough to meet a 'pilgrim' on the Upland Way. Most people do the walk from west to east, and many of them are only too ready for a chat, having just completed a very lonely part of their journey. The last time my wife and I did this walk, we met a charming Irishman, who, while passing the time of day, told us we were the first people he had met since setting out five days before. Having walked the length and breadth of the country, he wondered why it had taken him so long to find such country as this. I judged him to have a good eye for beauty, but felt loath to tell him that after the Moffat Hills the Southern Upland Way becomes very ordinary.

The fence keeps you company as you descend the gentle slopes through the gate in the dyke, and on to the farm track near Bogg cottage. Turn right on to the track which takes you back to your car.

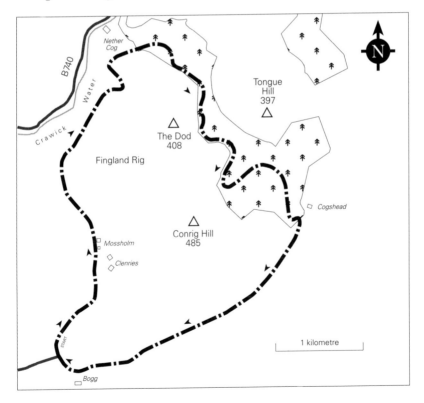

Auchenleck Hill

Allowing for a leisurely lunch break, this 14-kilometre walk should take just under 4 hours. O.S. map 78, starting point: 942977.

This is, in my opinion, one of the most rewarding walks in Nithsdale. Although there isn't a lot of climbing in the circuit, on a fine sunny day such as we had, the scenery is varied and outstanding.

After what had seemed a very long winter, it was cheering to see that, at long last, spring was with us. The sun shone out of a clear sky, defying the weather man's dismal forecast. As if to reinforce our hopes, a skylark, that classic harbinger of spring, rose nearby.

Our intention was to walk round Auchenleck Hill, one of the Durisdeer group, lying in Upper Nithsdale. Those hills seem to have a lot of character, cradling the wee village in their midst. To get to our starting point, we had driven along the narrow road that leads out northwest through Ae Forest (from the A701 at Parkgate), past Mitchellslacks and Locherben, and parked at the bridge that carries the track into Garroch farm.

After crossing the bridge, we walked over the flat meadow ahead to pick up the track that starts beside a solitary sandstone gatepost. The track follows Garroch Water, crossing and recrossing it as you keep to the valley floor. On the left the ridge of Auchenleck Hill rises gently up to its heather-clad summit. Over to the right rises Wester Hill. The track becomes more pronounced now – evidence of its use by hunters, for here we are in the heart of grouse-shooting country. Looking across at the thickly heathered slopes of Auchenleck Hill, we made out a line of shooting butts stretching up the slope. The heather was obviously well managed: patches of alternate years' burning stood out. Our path was climbing now, taking us past the skirts of The Dod, with Garroch Fell looming up behind.

Now we were descending, the track taking us down to meet Berry Grain as it tumbled out of the cleft between Garroch Fell and its source high up on Wedder Law. We paused to watch two buzzards circle over the slopes of Garroch. Having gone out through the gate, we changed direction, skirting White Snout to our left.

Down in the valley, we picked up the burn as it flowed into the deep defile of Cample Cleuch between the steep northern flank of Auchenleck Hill (Black Snout) and the one with the intriguing name, Bellybought Hill. The burn, and its accompanying path, proved to be a veritable sun trap; the series of small falls and delightful pools formed as it tumbled down through the cleft made it a most attractive place to linger, so we settled down beside one of the many pools for a spot of lunch. Incidentally, I'm led to believe that at the turn of the century this was thought to be an excellent trout stream.

The path runs sometimes above and sometimes down by the burn, and should be treated with care, especially in wet weather: it wouldn't be difficult to turn an ankle here. Emerging from the defile, at its southern end, you come on the first of the large cairns around here (the rest are on the other side of the valley over on the slopes of Auchenleck Hill, where they indicate a route up to the summit). At this point you have a choice of routes. You can follow the cairns up to the top of the hill, over and back to the car, or you can follow the dyke that runs parallel with the cairns, keeping it to your right, back to the start. The third option is to walk out to Burn farm and take the road back round to the car. We opted for the latter to avoid disturbing the grouse (nesting time was approaching) and the ewes, who were busy lambing.

Before heading off over the slopes towards the farm, we spent some time watching the antics of six wild goats doing a balancing act on top of a dyke before scampering effortlessly up the rocky face of Auchenleck Hill.

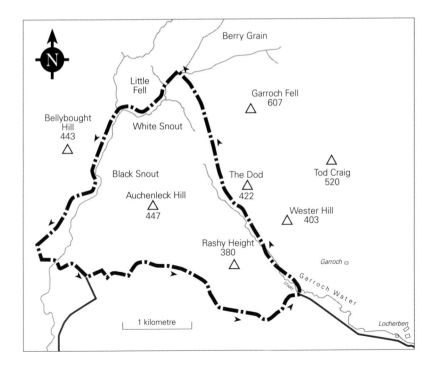

We now had fine views of the countryside surrounding Durisdeer, with Morton Castle standing out against the trees. No wonder Dorothy Wordsworth, her brother William, and Samuel Coleridge were impressed when they journeyed between Thornill and Wanlockhead on an August day back in 1803. Dorothy wrote in her diary, 'View pleasant down the river towards Thornhill' and 'An open country, corn fields, pastures and scattered trees'; she also remarked on the clay cottages that dotted the route every quarter mile. Well, the dwellings may have changed, but the countryside seems much the same.

Usually a long, flat stretch on tarmac at the end of a day spent in the hills has a way of taking the icing off the cake. But this walk proved to be the exception, for as the road wound round and back to our car, the scenery was ever-changing. We were presented with fine views out over Thornhill to the hills round Penpont and Moniaive. Near the end of the walk, we could see over to Dunscore in one direction and study the profiles of Queensberry and Wee Queensberry over to our left.

Durisdeer Village.

JUNE

O' my Luve's like a red red rose
That's newly sprung in June
O' my Luve's like the melodie
That's sweetly played in tune.

Robert Burns

Walking over by Durisdeer

These Durisdeer hills, less demanding than others, are still well worth a visit. 4 hours would be more than ample for this pleasurable, but not too strenuous, outing of 9 kilometres. O.S. map 78, starting point: 894038.

The Queensberry Marbles may not be among the Seven Wonders of the World – in fact to me, they are so ornate as to be slightly vulgar. But for a tiny village such as Durisdeer, they are quite an attraction. The statues represent James, Duke of Queensberry, and his Duchess. In the vault beneath the marbles lie the coffins of twelve Douglases, ranging in date from 1693 to 1777.

Durisdeer, nestling amongst the Lowthers and near the Dalveen Pass (A702), was not always such a sleepy wee place. Although the population is now about seventeen, just over a century ago it approached one hundred; many of the inhabitants were weavers.

The church and the village itself were resting places for the numerous pilgrims, among them, James IV of Scotland, to Whithorn and St Ninian's in Galloway.

Leaving the car beside the church, we set off through the gate opposite and followed the track up the glen, with Durisdeer Rig rising on our right and Black Hill over to our left, a route that offers an ideal start to a hill day – a gentle beginning, but gaining height all the time. Two buzzards circled lazily over Well Hill, no doubt keeping a wary eye on us.

Arriving at the gate and double fence at the county boundary, we left the path to wend its way over to Elvanfoot and started, instead, to climb the steep slopes of Durisdeer Hill, keeping the fence on our right and heading south. The hillside is pockmarked with hundreds of rabbit warrens, and the dogs engaged in a fruitless uphill chase in pursuit of a hare that rose close by. This chap was a bit unusual as he was almost completely black.

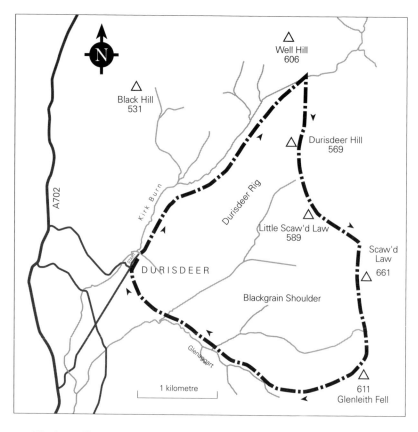

Having climbed up to the summit of Durisdeer Hill, we walked along the gently ascending ridge on to Little Scaw'd Law, then Scaw'd Law itself. Lunch was taken sheltering behind the dyke, at the point where it changes direction and sets off towards distant Wedder Law. As we sat munching our sandwiches and contentedly taking in the view, we were startled by the sight of a large black shape in the sky above a neighbouring hill top. As we watched, the shape ebbed and flowed, constantly changing and at times even seeming to roll down the edge of the hill on the skyline. It eventually dawned on us that it was a huge flock of thousands of birds wheeling about over the hill tops. I'm told it was possibly a large flock of starlings performing an aerobatic movement called an evolution. There seems no satisfactory explanation for why they do this, though it is said sometimes to be provoked by the sighting of a predator. If anybody has any suggestions of any other likely species which could have been flying in such numbers at two thousand feet, I'd be glad to hear from them. It was an astonishing spectacle.

After lunch, we climbed over the dyke and headed south again on to Glenleith Fell. There we found the first cairn of the day: a small one really. It's nice to see these hills mainly unspoiled by cairns which, in my opinion, stick out like ugly warts on an otherwise weathered face. Why some people get the urge to erect piles of stones on the way up, or on the summit of every hill they climb, beats me. Here the hills are for the moment pretty quiet, though the numerous discarded cartridge cases and well-managed heather show that they are obviously shot over.

Dropping down over the heathery slopes of Glenleith, heading for the burn that runs down Glenaggart, we could see Kettleton Reservoir cradled in the hills to the south west. We descended to the bottom of the valley, next to the shepherd's house. This is where you turn north-west and follow the track all the way back to the village. Somewhere along the track are more sites of Roman camps.

Make sure you pay a visit to the small church standing in the centre of the village. Built in the late seventeenth century, it stands on the site of an earlier one with records of ministers going back to 1394, when a certain John de Cader was in the pulpit. It's a wee kirk with plenty of history in it and even has its own Martyr's Grave containing the remains of a Covenanter named Daniel McMichael, who was shot by Sir John Dalziel at Lower Dalveen farm, nearby.

However I suppose what attracts most visitors to the church are the Queensberry Marbles, and I'll leave you to decide what you think of them. Actually, what impressed me most were the box pews which I had never seen before.

The Wanlockhead Circuit

This walk, of 13.5 kilometres, should take just under 4 hours to complete. O.S. map 78, starting point: 875131.

This walk follows a loop of the Southern Upland Way. Although it is relatively short, parts of the route are fairly exposed, so take plenty of stout clothing.

Lying at almost 460 metres in the Lowther Hills, the little village of Wanlockhead is the highest in Scotland. It can therefore also boast the highest pub and restaurant. For over three centuries, this was a centre of gold, silver and lead mining, and the Wanlockhead Mining Museum and partially restored railway line are well worth a visit. The last mine was shut down in the mid-'thirties, and the original railway line closed at the outbreak of the Second World War.

Today amateur prospectors pan for gold in the streams and recently the World Gold Panning Competition was held here. The gold for the crowns of Scotland was mined from the hills around this wee village.

We left our car in the car park at the museum, resisting the temptation to go into the attractive tearoom for a cuppa. With the museum on our right, we took the tarmac road and kept a look out for the Upland Way sign. It was not too long before we came on the Lochnell Mine, over to our left, which was in operation in 1710.

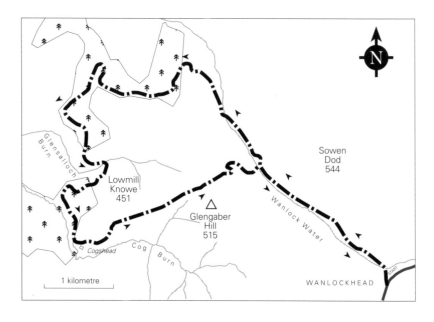

As we left the village, heading north-west, we took a look at the impressive beam engine, which was used to pump water from the workings of the Margaret and Straight Step Mines in the early years of the last century. Before the beam engine was installed, water had been cleared by the use of a pump called a horse gin, which involved a horse walking round driving a huge drum. Most of the mines in this locality were exploiting a seam of lead that stretched the width of the valley.

Last time I was there, it was a dour day with heavy skies and a threat of rain – just right for a low-level walk, and posing no problems of navigation, even for me. I suppose it was the subdued mood of the day that prompted us to visit the graveyard just outside the village on the left side of the road. One would expect the life expectancy of the miners to have been low, but I was surprised to discover that many lived to a ripe old age. There was of course the usual high number of infant mortalities that you see in all old churchyards.

Just past here, the tarmac runs out, and we found ourselves on a track leading past more recent mine workings on our right. Just under Glengaber Hill we reached the start of the loop designed into the Way. Here you can choose in which direction to do the walk: either clockwise, in which case you cross Wanlock Water by the bridge on your left, or anti-clockwise in which case you press straight on. We chose the latter and followed the track round the hillside. The weather cleared, and our spirits rose. As we drew away from the stark greyness of the old workings, the scenery became more attractive. The gradient was kindly, and the path plunged in and out of clumps of trees, making for a pleasant and varied route.

As we approached the second planting, where the path crosses the hillside above Glensalloch Burn, we were lucky enough to witness nature at work. A strong wind had risen, and we could see beneath us the moisture from the wet conifers being driven through the valley and upwards in a great cloud. It's unusual to witness such a graphic demonstration of rainwater being reabsorbed into the atmosphere.

Our path took a final dive into the trees and brought us out at the ruined steading at Cogshead. Here the Way drops down into Sanquhar and eventually goes on to Port Patrick. We weren't going that far, so we followed the loop north-eastwards on to the open hill. Upland Way signs led us through the mire, over the narrow bridge spanning Cog Burn and through the gate in the electric fence.

Nearing the summit of Glengaber Hill, we were entertained by two ravens performing their tumbling act. The largest of the crow family, the raven performs spectacular aerial manoeuvres during the mating season in the spring. At times a bird will fly upside down, then suddenly lose height in a vertical dive. With the decrease of sheep in the hills, the raven population has also declined, as the bird is dependent on sheep carrion for part of its diet. The path took us gently back to the bridge over Wanlock Water.

The beam engine at Wanlockhead.
New rolling stock at Leadhills Station.

The glowing ruby should adorn
Those who in warm July are born.

Anonymous

Ettrick Pen and Bodesbeck Ridge

Although the short grass and heather make for easy going underfoot, allow about 6 hours for this 15-kilometre walk. O.S. map 79, starting point: 183088.

A spell of fine hot weather, although welcomed by sun worshippers, is sometimes greeted with mixed feelings by the hillwalker. While it may be dry overhead and underfoot, a long day spent in the hills under a blazing sun can be pretty tiring.

So my wife and I were not unduly perturbed when we left the car at Potburn under grey, overcast skies. Potburn farm can be found by turning off the B709 at Ettrick and heading west along the narrow road past the monument on the birthplace of James Hogg (*see* The Captain's Road, page 30).

Looking east down Black Hope glen from Whirly Gill.

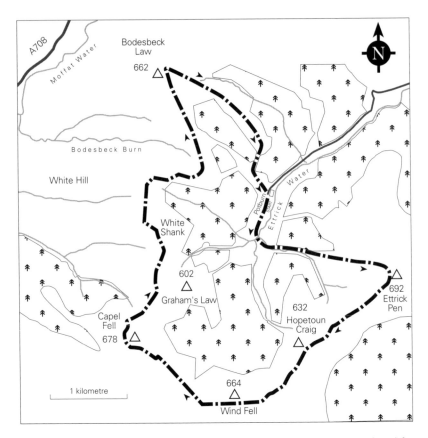

Hogg's first publication was a miscellany of verse under the title *Mountain Bard* (1807). Unfortunately he invested the proceeds of this, and another book on sheep management, *The Shepherd's Guide* (also 1807), in an ill-fated venture on a farm in Dumfriesshire. Hogg finally left for Edinburgh, there to make his living by writing. He was sponsored by the then Duke of Buccleuch, who set him up in a small farm in Yarrow.

Walk south along the track from Potburn, then cross Ettrick Water by the bridge at Over Phawhope, passing the bothy on your right and heading east along the path before climbing the slopes of Ettrick Pen. By the time we reached this point, the sun had burned off the cloud, and we could feel the heat building. After clearing Ettrick Pen's cairned summit, we followed the fence (the old county boundary) over to Hopetoun Craig and then on to Wind Fell.

Lunch was to be delayed until our next peak, Capel Fell. This involves a steep, knee-cracking descent to Ettrick Head, where the route crosses the Southern Upland Way. (By now, it was stiflingly hot, and there was no cooling breeze in the valley.) I always feel that here the planners of the Upland Way, by keeping to the valley floor as it enters Ettrick, have shown very little imagination. It would have been far more attractive to have followed the heights of the Bodesbeck Ridge all the way to Herman Law and on over the hill to Ettrick in the east.

After lunch on top of Capel Fell, we enjoyed this rather unfamiliar view of the Moffat Hills and engaged in a bout of summit naming. Stretched out on the warm dry grass, we gazed drowsily up at the clear sky; above us a couple of kestrels hovered and a buzzard wheeled lazily on the warm air currents. My mind drifted back to an August day, every bit as warm, during the long, dry, hot summer of 1984. That day we had underestimated just how warm it was going to be. Our two dogs were suffering quite a bit, due to the heat and the lack of water. We had to stamp in the damp, peaty hags to encourage water to come to the surface, so that the dogs could get at least a little brackish water. So distressed was one of them that my wife took a short-cut back to get her out of the sun. Shortly after, as the remaining dog and I made our way down into the valley, manna appeared in the form of a deep, cool rock pool, and man and dog plunged in together, in the altogether, to their mutual relief.

Reluctantly stirring ourselves from our reverie, we left the summit and walked over the short grass to White Shank. Here one loses height, dropping well down before climbing up alongside the fence to Bodes-beck Law. From this point, there is a choice of routes. The walk can be extended by continuing along the ridge to Herman Law, which, on a clear day, is well worth doing as the views are so good, then you can retrace your steps to Bodesbeck for the final part of the walk. Altern-atively, you can do as we did and head down south-eastwards towards Potburn taking the path between forestry plantations. We arrived at the same pool in the Longhope Burn where we had bathed eight years before. This time we merely dipped our hot feet gingerly in its chilly waters.

Walking the Marches

This long and fairly arduous walk of about 22 kilometres, with much ascent and rough terrain, requires two cars or an obliging chauffeur. Allow 6 to 7 hours. O.S. maps 78 and 79, starting point: 056127; finishing point: 233160.

Leave your car at the entrance to the conifer plantation above the Devil's Beef Tub on the eastern side of the A701, taking care not to block the gateway.

Until well into the 17th century, the English made frequent forays into Annandale. It fell to the Warden of the Western Marches to ride the boundaries (the Marches) and ensure that they were unbreached. This tradition is still marked today in the many galas or Ridings of the Marches held each year in Scottish border towns. This walk echoes the tradition and follows the old Dumfriesshire boundary where it met the counties of Peeblesshire and Selkirk.

Before you start, take a look a few hundred metres down the road towards Moffat at the small stone which commemorates the shooting of a fleeing Covenanter on the slopes of Great Hill opposite.

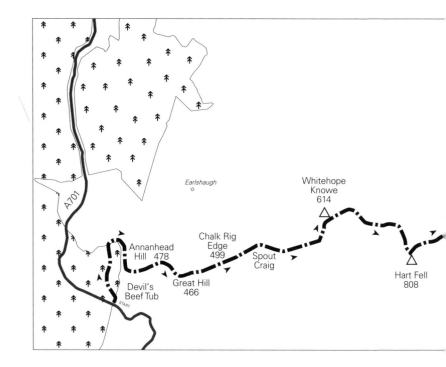

The starting point for the walk is high above the steep-sided slopes of the Devil's Beef Tub, also known as the Earl of Annandale's Larder, being a convenient place to hide stolen English cattle. Follow the track into the forest heading north until you reach a fence at its northern edge and the open hillside. The fence marks the county boundary and you will follow it for the whole walk until you get to the A708 above Birkhill. Before doing so, have a look in the grass on the left-hand side of the track which leads towards Tweedshaws farm. About 30 metres along it, you should find a small, square stone. The track was originally the route of the road to Edinburgh, and the stone marks the spot where the guard's body was found after the mailcoach foundered in a blizzard in 1831.

Keep to the edge of the forest and walk east round to the summit of Annanhead Hill – the first top of the day – then skirt Great Hill. 1½ kilometres to the north lies the derelict steading, Earlshaugh.

The route leads along the edge of the Beef Tub, with fine views down into the valley of Annandale. After you cross Chalk Rig Edge, there is some rough ground to negotiate before you step over one of the tiny burns that feed the infant River Annan at its source, deep down in the Tub. At this point the fence becomes rather broken down; the

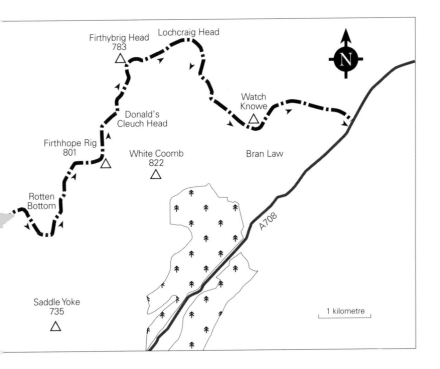

next summit is White Hope Knowe to the north-east. Unfortunately, after this, we have to lose height, dropping down into the valley, before the fence ascends to the top of Hart Fell.

A ridge take us gently over to Hartfell Rig, above Saddle Craigs. Here the walk becomes fairly demanding as the fence leads over some (usually) wet ground, skirting Rotten Bottom, and up to Firthhope Rig.

A relatively easy stretch now follows as we keep to the high ground, over Donald's Cleuch Head and on to Firthybrig Head. More wet ground ahead, though, as we go downhill again before climbing up the steep side of Lochcraig Head. Once there, however, it all seems worthwhile: we are rewarded with a superb view of Loch Skeen far below.

It's a knee-jarring descent following the dyke and fence off Lochcraig Head, and you may well find, as we did, that there are some pretty wet peat hags to be negotiated as you walk the length of Loch Skeen along its eastern bank and then climb up on to Watch Knowe. The area is one in which the Covenanters held outdoor religious services, and this hill's name is a reminder that it was once used as a vantage point from which to spot any approaching dragoons. From Watch Knowe it's fairly easy going; just keep the fence company until you reach the A708 just above Birkhill cottage, and pray that your chauffeur is waiting.

Near the Devil's Beef Tub, with Hart Fell beckoning.

Muckle Knees

This is not a long walk (9 kilometres), but, considering the rough terrain involved, quite demanding. It took me just under 3½ hours. That included lunch and three striptease acts. O.S. map 79, starting point: 197155.

A strong wind buffeted the car as I drove north on the A74. In no time the sky darkened, and the wipers worked furiously to keep the screen clear. Dark clouds pressed angrily against the western flanks of the Moffat Hills, and Hart Fell receded into a gloomy, ominous murk. It was about now that I began to have second thoughts about the whole venture, wondering whether this really was the kind of day to be making my first acquaintance with Muckle Knees. As the forecast had been for 'Showers, heavy at times, mainly in the west', I decided to press on. Anyway, Muckle Knees was to be found to the east.

I'd better explain. I wasn't setting out to meet a sturdy-legged fellow hillwalker with a penchant for walking the hills in shorts. I was going to visit for the first time yet another of those Southern Upland Hills with slightly odd names; close by Muckle Knees are Nickies Knowe and Dead for Cauld.

In spite of its 588 metres, Muckle Knees doesn't have a very interesting or dramatic summit. However, for anyone acquainted with the hills surrounding Loch Skeen, it affords a new and interesting view of these hills, lying in the wild desolate land between Moffat and Yarrow.

Driving up through the valley of Moffat Water, I congratulated myself on not turning back, for it seemed that the further east I went, the brighter it became. I parked the car in the lay-by just short of Birkhill, where Raking Gill tumbles steeply off Bodesbeck Ridge and then flows under the road and down to meet Moffat Water.

Having scrambled down the slope on the north side of the road and over the burn, I followed the ridge up to my right, skirting the deep gash of what is known as Dob's Linn and going as far as the fence which marks the old county boundaries of Dumfries and Selkirk and now the bounds of National Trust land. This fence runs all the way up to the summit of Watch Knowe and eventually on to the top of Lochcraig Head. I followed it to just short of Watch Knowe summit. By now the wind was so strong that it was all I could do to avoid being blown on to the fence.

It was almost a relief to change direction, get the wind on my back, and follow another fence heading off to the north. Here, there is supposed to be a path taking you on over the summmit of The Strypes. It's certainly hard to find, and I found the going quite demanding as

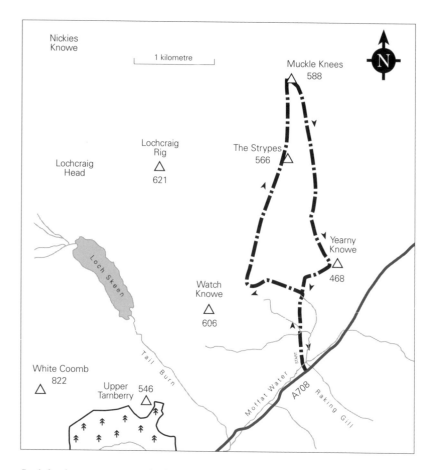

I picked my way round about and over the peat hags. Mind you, the effort was well worth it: the views were magnificent. Looking back over my left shoulder I got really unusual views of Lochcraig Head and White Coomb, and a really precipitous angle on the ridge of Donald's Cleuch Head. Approaching Muckle Knees, I was rewarded with a fine view of the ridge leading up from the Megget Stone and on over into Moffat Dale. Out through the gap in the hills I could just make out the tip of Megget Reservoir, gleaming blue in the sunlight, with the hills of Manor and Tweed as a backdrop.

Lunch was eaten sheltering from the cold wind behind a rather low peat hag. The sky darkened as the weather moved east bringing a sudden icy squall howling round my rather meagre shelter, so it was on with the waterproofs. My intention was to cut across the rough ground, over the top of Yearny Knowe, heading back to the road at

Birkhill. Not knowing how long this squall would last I thought it wise to take a compass bearing before tackling the peat hags. This was hurriedly done, compass and map were crammed deeply into anorak pockets followed by hands, and I cooried doon, hoping the storm would soon pass.

It cleared as quickly as it had arrived and I was able to savour the landscape once again bathed in sunlight before setting out across the hags. Such was the weather that I had to don and remove my water-proofs three times on the way. There were two burns (Kerrcleuch and Happerbutie Burns) to negotiate before reaching the fence above Birkhill and following the ridge back round to Dob's Linn.

On returning to my car I spoke to some amateur geologists, a young couple and their daughter, who were off into Dob's Linn in search of graptolites. Seemingly on their last visit they had found two, and were now well and truly bitten by the fossil-hunting bug.

Daer Reservoir from Watchman's Brae.

If the twenty-fourth of August be fair and clear
Then hope for a prosperous Autumn that year.

John Ray (17th century)

Daer

Allow about 5 hours for this 13-kilometre walk. O.S. map 78, starting and finishing point: 966068.

The plaintive call of the curlew was loud as my wife and I parked the car beside the reservoir. Daer's waters sparkled as the sun dappled the ripples made by the light breeze. The whaups wheeled and counter wheeled above our heads, then swooped out over the hills on the far shore.

To find the starting point for this walk, drive north up the M74 and leave it at Elvanfoot (for access from the north, take the turning to

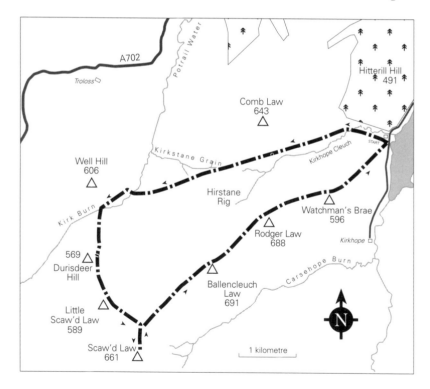

Crawford). Follow the A702 for about three miles until you see Daer Reservoir signposted to the left; take this narrow road, which leads through the farm of Nunnerie. Before you reach the dam, take the right fork through the forest, hugging the west shore of the reservoir. Park your car just beyond the shepherd's cottage, where the forest ends. We had been hoping to find a path which we had spotted on the rather ancient 1:50,000 First Series O.S. map; it was supposed to lead over the hill to join up with the Roman road running from Durisdeer to Elvanfoot, and we had it in mind to return over the tops to the car. But our attempts to trace it proved both fruitless and frustrating, so the following is probably a better plan.

From the lay-by, follow the fence which contours the northern slopes of Watchman's Brae leading away from the reservoir above the sheep pens, then drop down to the old pens near the Kirkhope Cleuch burn. After crossing the burn, you follow a rather indistinct path along its northern bank. Hereabouts the going is quite demanding, as the ground is pretty rough, although it improves near the top.

We headed for the bealach between Comb Law and Hirstane Rig. Near the top, the burn forks; we took the right fork on to the bealach. Standing on the top we were able to see down into the next valley, and finally spotted the Roman road clearly following the valley floor, just beyond Kirk Burn.

A couple of oystercatchers became quite agitated by our arrival, concerned lest we disturb their young by the side of the burn. Our route of descent involved dropping down into the valley and joining the road about a kilometre south-west of where Kirkstane Grain runs into Kirk Burn. We followed the Roman road up again in a south-westerly direction to the dyke, which, besides separating two farms, marks the old boundary between Dumfriesshire and Lanarkshire.

It is said that in Roman times a detachment of troops was stationed nearby to keep the local Selgovae tribe in order. In those days, this area would have been covered in light forest; in fact the name Durisdeer derives from the Celtic meaning 'the door to the forest'.

During the Killing Times, one of the most famous Covenanters dwelt not far from here. Elias Wilson, his wife and young child lived in a cottage on Dalveen farm. Elias's Covenanter sympathies inevitably became known to the authorities, who dispatched a troop of dragoons, under the command of an officer and a sergeant to arrest him. Fortunately, Elias got word of their approach, and he and his wife and child hurried to the safety of a cave high up on a steep hillside at Enterkin, a nearby pass. When the dragoons arrived to apprehend him, Elias refused to come out of the cave, so the sergeant made to climb up to the cave's entrance. Elias promptly took aim and shot the sergeant dead, who fell against the other officer causing him, too, to plunge to his death in the ravine below. So Elias got two dragoons for the price of one musket ball. After darkness had fallen, the family crept out of the cave unobserved and made their escape.

Things seemed a bit more peaceful as we set ourselves the steep climb up the slopes of Durisdeer Hill to achieve before lunch. Before starting, we paused to admire the large patches of wild thyme blanketing the sides of Well Hill behind us.

The rather taxing climb was well worth it. We were rewarded with some fine views into Nithsdale from our lunch stop behind the dyke on Scaw'd Law. Seen from this vantage point, the countryside round Drumlanrig looked exceptionally lush. We gazed down on a patchwork of greens and browns, with the Galloway Hills providing a dramatic backdrop.

After lunch we headed north-east, following the fence, up over Ballencleuch Law and on up the next slope towards Rodger Law. This is a fine broad ridge, with a fairly moderate incline. The views opened out all round us. Over to the east, we were presented with an unusual view of the Moffat Hills, the great cleft at the Spa making Hart Fell easily identifiable. Behind lurked White Coomb with Carrifran Gans peeping coyly over its shoulder. In the far distance to the south, one could make out the hazy outline of the Lake District Peaks beyond the glistening Solway Firth.

Approaching the summit of Rodger Law, we were intrigued to see a large flock of rooks performing the aerobatic movement known as an evolution. On our last visit to these hills, we had seen the same thing executed by what we took to be a flock of starlings. There must be something about these hills which encourages birds to perform in this way. I can't say I've noticed it elsewhere.

Descending gradually over Watchman's Brae we arrived back at the car. This is a very pleasant circuit, and, providing the weather obliges, it affords some splendid views.

Dalveen to Daer and back

This walk is fairly strenuous, and, with a leisurely break for lunch, takes just under 6 hours. You cover a little over 19 kilometres, but the variety of scenery makes for a memorable day out. O.S. map 78, starting point: 928095.

Like the last walk, this one takes us to the Lowther Hills and into country policed at one time by the Roman legions and later used by the Covenanters as a sanctuary. Our route leads out of the strath above the Dalveen Pass and, following the Upland Way, over to Daer, and then back over the hills west of Daer to return to the car.

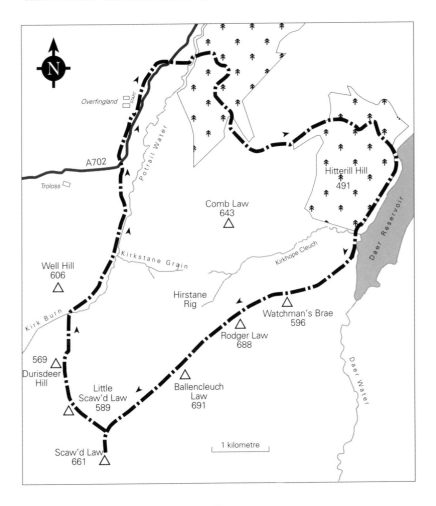

Driving down the A702 from the north, you pass Peden cottage and Peden Burn (there was a Covenanting preacher of the same name). It is said that this part of the Lowthers was not so strictly policed by the dragoons and thus witnessed unusually open activity by the Covenanters.

We parked the car in a lay-by on the A702 near Overfingland. We picked up the Southern Upland Way several hundred metres to the north-east where it leaves the road and heads east, and followed it over meadows and across the bridge spanning Potrail Water. The signposted Upland Way now strikes up into a mature conifer plantation leading over towards Daer, and it occurred to me that on a hot day the flies would be murder; however, we survived unmolested. A broad track makes for easy and very pleasant walking through the tall trees and eventually you come out into open country allowing a glimpse of the houses over by the dam at Daer.

Leading back into the forest, the track then skirts Hitteril Hill and eventually comes to a junction. The Upland Way is signposted to the left, but our route heads off to the right. Joining the road which runs alongside Daer Reservoir, the surface now turns to tarmac. No great hardship, though, for we walk only as far as the foot of Watchman's Brae, just beyond Kirkhope Cleuch and the cottage.

There is then a pull up the face of Watchman's Brae, probably the steepest part of the route, and on to the summit where there is a rather unusual stone summit marker. Time now to pause for breath and look down upon the bare summit of Hitteril Hill above its thickly wooded flanks – a bit reminiscent of a monk's tonsure. Time also to reflect on the name of the hill we're on: probably yet another Covenanters' lookout spot. For here we're right in the heart of Covenanting country. Not far away, to the south-west, lies the wee village of Durisdeer with its own martyr's grave in the kirkyard. And just over at Dalveen lived Elias Wilson, a Covenanter noted for his daring escape from the dragoons (*see* page 79, Daer).

Perhaps the most famous escape or rescue in this area took place over at Enterkin in August 1684. Daniel Defoe (author of *Robinson Crusoe*) gives one account of the event. A minister and five other Covenanters were being escorted by dragoons through the pass at Enterkin on their way to Edinburgh to stand trial. Suddenly, out of the mists above the party, twelve horsemen appeared and surrounded the group. On hearing their demand that the prisoners be released immediately, the dragoon captain, a gent named Kelte, foolishly refused. He was promptly shot in the head, whereupon the rest of his men quickly agreed to the release of the prisoners. He nevertheless achieved the doubtful honour of having a nearby waterfall named after him –

Kelte's Linn. The Government, stunned by the audacity of the rescue, was quick and savage in its response. Instructions were issued for every male in Nithsdale over the age of fifteen to be brought in for questioning. Claverhouse had the reputation of assembling children as young as six years old and ordering his dragoons to fire muskets over their heads to induce them to provide information.

After pushing on over Watchman's Brae we climbed up to the summit of Rodger Law with its newly erected radio mast. Unfortunately for us, the skies darkened and the mist rolled in accompanied by heavy rain, denying us the superb views normally available as you walk along the broad ridge towards Ballencleuch Law. Once on top of Ballencleuch Law, you have the option to shorten the walk and head off to the north-west in the direction of the Roman road. We decided to take the longer alternative and to follow the fence in a south-westerly direction along and up to the dyke near Scaw'd Law's summit.

Turning our backs to the driving rain we set off downhill, now to the north-west, keeping company with the dyke on our left. This took us over Little Scaw'd Law, Durisdeer Hill and steeply down to the old Roman road. Turn north-east along the Roman road about three kilometres from Durisdeer (where the Romans had a fort from which to keep the local Selgovae tribes in order). Tramping along in the rain, I wondered how the soldiers compared this posting with the sun-baked plains of Tuscany or the south of France.

The track following the old Roman road leads away from Durisdeer and along towards Elvanfoot. On reaching the sheep pens a short distance from Troloss farm, ignore the path to the steading on your left and follow the track up side of the conifer plantation and back up to the main road. Then turn right and walk back to your car.

The Sheep Stealers' Trail

This is quite a demanding walk of about 22 kilometres, which takes just over 6 hours, but the beauty of the scenery makes the distance fly by. O.S. map 78, starting point: 050024.

I started with a quest in mind: to find the memorial stone which I suspected lay somewhere in the vicinity of the Southern Upland Way along its Beattock stretch.

One of three stones which had interested me for nearly a year, I had finally resolved to do something about locating the two I had not yet seen. One of the stones is the small red sandstone block which marks the place where the body of the guard on the ill-fated Edinburgh Royal Mail coach was found above the Beef Tub in 1831 (*see* page 73).

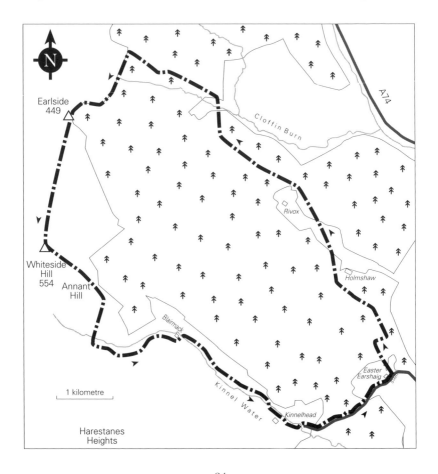

The second was erected in memory of an unfortunate young gent named Fraser, who expired in 1753 after consuming too much drink and food on an expedition to Loch Skeen. The third commemorates the hanging in 1795 of John Johnston for the not-uncommon offence of sheep stealing.

Well, I've seen the first one, and a reader of my newspaper articles kindly gave me directions on how to find the second, but the stone commemorating the sheep stealer was proving just a wee bit elusive. Old records told me that it lies in the march dyke between Kinnelhead's Cairn or Stane Hill and Holmshaw. But all that area now lies deeply blanketed by forestry.

However, I still felt it was worth a try, as the search could be combined with a walk along an attractive part of the Southern Upland Way followed by a tramp back round the forest over the hill. As it happened, my search for the stone proved fruitless, but we were more than recompensed by a find near the end of our walk.

The day promised heat as we drove up the Crooked Road out of Beattock village (the turning opposite Beattock House Hotel) and parked our car in the car park just short of Easter Earshaig.

Walking a short distance towards the farm buildings we soon picked up the Upland Way sign, then struck off across a field and into the forest. It is not long before you come upon a magnificent wee lochan set jewel-like in an idyllic forest clearing. The place just begs you to linger, but we had to resist the temptation as we had a good few kilometres ahead of us. The Upland Way took us out through the forest, with signposted paths going off in all directions until eventually we reached a clearing near Holmshaw.

Here we came on the remains of the march dyke, and I searched hopefully for the stone. No luck – the forest had closed in, engulfing much of the dyke. I must confess that we were not too worried, as the walk itself was proving so enjoyable. We walked on into the clearing at Holmshaw, crossed the Foy Bridge and headed for the next stage which would take us up through the forest past Rivox then on towards Brattleburn.

We ate our lunch in the sunshine not far from a small bothy which looked almost like some Alpine chalet set in a clearing in the forest. In the beautiful weather we had been blessed with, this part of the Upland Way was indeed oddly reminiscent of the French Alps.

Beside us, the Cloffin Burn tumbled noisily out beneath the track into a deep pool before rushing off down towards Middlegill through a gully lined thickly with rowan trees and willows. The dogs swam in the cool waters of the pool while the humans looked on with envy.

Reluctantly, we left this spot and crossed the track leading into Brattleburn. Our route took us steeply up towards the end of the forest on the distant skyline. Time now to stop frequently to look back over the immense stretch of forest towards Annandale and the Moffat Hills.

Reaching the end of the forest we now gazed over desolate moorland towards the Lowthers proper, while beneath us lay Daer with Lowther Hill in the background. The Upland Way turns to the right at this point before swinging down towards the dam, while our route took us to the left, round the outside of the forest.

Walking across peat hags can be pretty hard going, so it is advisable to follow the faint track on the forest side of the fence. When the trees close in, cross the fence and if you look carefully you can find a somewhat indistinct path round the edge of the forest. It's quite a long trek, so if the ground is reasonably dry, it is worth cutting across from Earlside to Whiteside Hill and then to Annant Hill. Dropping down off the steep slopes of Hoarlaw, we arrived at Kinnel Water and crossed the rather rickety bridge close to the edge of the forest. From here, it's down the track and out past the steading of Blairmack. There is then quite a long walk on tarmac before you reach Kinnelhead farm.

Here we were lucky enough to meet an old acquaintance, Kinnelhead's shepherd, Paul. Always the enthusiast, Paul told us of his current passion for road- and mountain-biking. He also has a fascination for, and a considerable knowledge of, the history of the large area in which he herds. We were told that he had indeed seen the stone, but many years ago, and that even then it had been well covered with moss. Seemingly we had been searching in the wrong area. So I decided to make one more attempt to find it, equipped with new clues from Paul.

Earlier in the day I had noticed a tower marked on the map at Kinnelhead, but I'd ignored it because I had never seen any sign of such a structure. As if to compensate us for missing the stone, Paul asked us if we would like to see the remains of the tower. We eagerly took him up on his offer. The find more than made up for not locating the stone. For here were the remains of a dwelling which dated back to the sixteenth century and probably further. Its overall shape and floor level were clearly visible; you could even make out the recess in the stonework which had carried the timber that barred the door. Nearby stood the cattle byre, complete with floor and water channel. What really caught our attention, though, were the faint but distinct traces of several small crosses carved into the rock of the tower. On another rock nearby was a cross which may even have been carved at the time of the Crusades. We went on our way, pleased at having renewed an acquaintance and delighted to have seen the Kinnelhead crosses. There remained a final tramp along the tarmac to get back to where we had parked the car.

If you are a plant enthusiast, there's plenty to see on this walk. We came on both the marsh and spotted varieties of orchid, bugle, hearts-ease, heath bedstraw, bilberry, birdsfoot-trefoil, cow-wheat and many others. You may also see foxes or roe deer or spot some of the many raptors and other birds which frequent the forest and nearby moorland.

Postscript

There is a happy ending to the story of my search for the Sheep Stealer's Stone. I did find it – thanks to Bob Armstrong who herded Blairmack for many years. Now retired, Bob had read my article in the *Dumfries and Galloway Standard* and 'phoned me up.

We found it up on the hill, in a clearing in the forest east of Blair-mack, at a spot marked Tannis Hill on the map. The flat stone lies on both sides of and straddled by the dyke – just at the corner where the dike changes direction to run north-east.

It was seriously mossed over and took a bit of finding. However my wife, displaying that innate skill possessed by the female of finding things left about by the male of the species, eventually scraped away the moss from a hump beneath the dyke to reveal the stone. We could faintly discern the words 'John Johnston' and the date '1795'.

Now, if the Mr Johnston mentioned on the stone was hanged for sheep stealing, it certainly wasn't from one of the current trees in the plantation – they are less than twenty years old. And maybe he didn't get his 'Jedart Justice' on this spot, but was executed elsewhere – this stone being merely a memorial to him. Just a short distance away stands Hangingshaw Hill. I will leave you to work this one out.

It's a private road from Kinnelhead up to Blairmack – so you can't drive up there. Either walk up the road to see where the stone is, or make it part of the Sheep Stealer's Trail, leave the walk's route at Blair-mack farm and walk up on to the hill from there. You will find the stone at grid ref. 019038.

A maiden born when Autumn leaves
Are rustling in September's breeze
A sapphire on her brow should bind
'Twill cure diseases of the mind.

Anonymous

Megget to Moffat

Allow just over 6 hours for this walk of 20 kilometres. O.S. Maps 72, 78 and 79, starting point: 153204 (back-up parking can be found at 092072).

This walk from Tweedsmuir over the tops to Moffat requires a fine day for easy navigation and good views.

We were dropped off at the Megget Stone and would have to 'hoof it' until we reached our back-up vehicle parked by the Well at Archbank farm, just above Moffat.

The Megget Stone stands at the summit of the narrow road which wends its way from Tweedsmuir, past Talla, climbing steeply out of the valley and descending past Megget Reservoir into Ettrick. The origin of the Stone is somewhat obscure. It may once have had some religious significance, but could merely have been a marker on the old county boundary between Peebles and Selkirk.

Looking back down the Megget valley, it's hard to imagine that this area was once part of the Royal Forest of Ettrick, hunted by Scottish monarchs up to the time of Mary Queen of Scots. The forest would have consisted of oaks and Scots pine – none of your firs and Sitka spruce and such-like modern rubbish. The stags running here were reputed to be the largest in Scotland, and beaters drove herds numbering in their thousands for the nobles to hunt.

Royal parties based themselves in Cramalt Tower, which was a hunting lodge in those days. Over on Talla Moss, according to the Ordnance Survey records for 1887, the horns of wild ox were found embedded in the peat. And at Fiend's Fell near Talla Linns, legend has it that eagles were at one time so numerous and aggressive that they tried to carry off a young shepherd boy. We gazed down on Talla and Megget Reservoirs which supply the drouthy citizens of Auld Reekie with water for their drams, but then pushed on, as there are quite a few kilometres of rough ground to cover between this spot and Moffat.

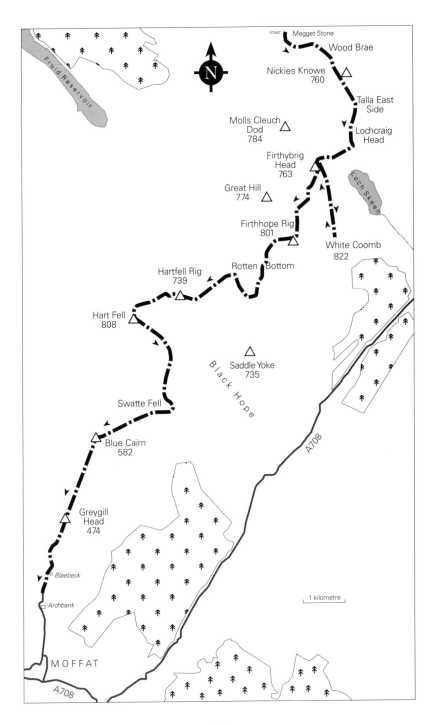

START Megget Stone

Wood Brae

Nickies Knowe
760

Talla East
Side

Lochcraig
Head

Molls Cleuch
Dod
784

Firthybrig
Head
763

Loch Skeen

Great Hill
774

Firthhope Rig
801

White Coomb
822

Rotten Bottom

Hartfell Rig
739

Hart Fell
808

Saddle Yoke
735

Black Hope

Swatte Fell

A708

Blue Cairn
582

Greygill
Head
474

Blaebeck

Archbank

Fruid Reservoir

N

1 kilometre

MOFFAT

A708

Looking down over Loch Skeen from the summit of Lochcraig Head.

After parking the car, we crossed the road, then headed due south over the rough ground until we reached the fence. This led us along over Wood Brae and up the steep flanks of Nickies Knowe, then south along the ridge, over Talla East Side, in the direction of Lochcraig Head. Following the fence and dyke along the ridge, someone remarks that it's a pity so many of the hill dykes round here have now fallen into disrepair when you think of all the hard work that must have gone into their building. I make a mental note to repeat this walk in snowy conditions, as this part looks really good for cross-country skiing.

We had just reached the summit of Lochcraig Head and below us lay Walter Scott's 'Dark Loch Skene, where eagles scream from shore to shore.' It's probably many years since eagles were here, and those lines paint a very sombre picture of this wee loch. To me, it has always seemed friendly in appearance and not in the least foreboding.

Standing on Lochcraig Head, we are on the tops now, and will probably maintain that height, except when we drop down into Rotten

Bottom. From our vantage point we can look over to the Eildon Hills in the east, far beyond Langholm to the Cheviots, out over Burnswark to the Lake District. Over to the west, Criffel guards the Solway tides backed by Screel and Bengairn. So with a light heart we follow the dyke to the south-west down the steep slope, up over Firthybrig Head and on to the top of White Coomb.

Retracing our steps off White Coomb, at the junction of the dykes south-west of Firthybrig Head, we followed the dyke heading off south-west down into Rotten Bottom. Now this is an area aptly named, just a place of peat bogs and hags which will sorely test the waterproof quality of your boots. We eventually slurped our soggy way out of there and back up on to the heights again, as we climbed Hartfell Rig and over to Hart Fell.

Here, the sheer joy of this walk is felt as you swing south-east off Hart Fell, along the Craigs high above Black Hope glen, with Saddle Yoke rising steeply out of its far side. For this is a walk of high tops and ridges, and to walk such ridges must be the ultimate among the many pleasures of hill-going. Looking down from the Craigs, high above the valley floor, I realised what is so special about these hills. They are dissected by long, steep-sided valleys which cleave right into the heart of the peaks and make them so dramatic.

After skirting the top of Swatte Fell, we left the ever-present fence to follow the heather-clad ridge south-west in a gentle descent to Moffat by way of Blue Cairn and Greygill Head.

By Glen Ea's Hill

This walk of 8 kilometres should take just over 3 hours, including a lunch break. O.S. Map 78, starting point map: 916164.

The walk starts in the vicinity of some of the old mines near the village of Leadhills. It takes you into grouse-shooting country – so give some thought to the timing of your expedition. The season starts on 'the Glorious Twelfth' (of August) and ends on 10th December.

After leaving the car in the lay-by on the B7040, I crossed over the road and forded Elvan Water. It was a beautiful crisp, autumn morning, with promise of fine views on top, as I took the stalkers' path up the

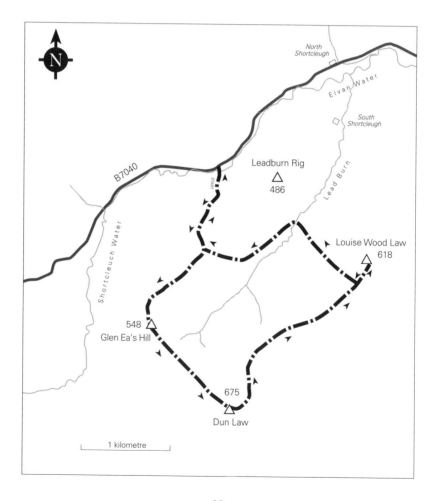

heathery slopes of Glen Ea's Hill. I passed two black sheds on my left. Above me a buzzard quartered the hillside in search of prey. Actually in the last few years things have been on the up and up for birds of prey, and their numbers are now quite high. Seemingly the poor wee vole holds the key to their success. Thankfully (though not for him), he was also around in large numbers.

Just beyond where the path finishes on the summit, you will find a rather ill-defined path leading over rough ground and up on to Dun Law. I missed it the first time and ended up following a line of shooting butts and picking up the path later. The pull up on to Dun Law is a touch monotonous.

Once on the summit, I had fine views all about and could see Daer Reservoir over to the south east. I followed the fence along the ridge towards the north east, dropping down nearly 100 metres before climbing up again on to White Law.

Next comes the moment of truth. To get up on to Louise Wood Law, the last hill on this walk, you have to drop steeply down into a gully and then climb out again on its far side. Here you have a choice: either take the path to the left of the screes which traverses the hill and then curves back to the summit, or follow the narrow path to the right of the screes beside the fence that goes straight up the hill. I chose the latter, as it was the shorter route.

On top of Louise Wood Law are a cairn and a trig point. Looking around for an easy descent, I took the gully that leads down to Lead Burn where there is a small yellow hut. Here the hillsides were covered by heather vainly trying to hold its bloom. Over on my left, the side of the gully was splashed with the ochre of autumn bracken.

Instead of following the glen out to South Shortcleugh farm, I walked up the Lead Burn towards its source. After about 500 metres I struck west across the skirts of Leadburn Rig, down among the rough peat hags, to rejoin the path at the two black sheds.

From here I retraced my steps on the path, then recrossed the river to reach my car. Incidentally, Elvan Water is the favoured haunt of gold prospectors, and you may be lucky enough (especially at the weekend) to see them panning the river for traces of gold.

Amang the bonie winding banks,
Where Doon rins, wimplin, clear;
Where Bruce ance ruled the martial ranks,
An' shook his Carrick spear;
Some merry, friendly, country-folks
Together did convene,
To burn their nits, an' pou their stocks,
An haud their Hallowe'en . . .

Robert Burns

Wamphray Glen

Allow just over 5 hours for this walk of 14 kilometres. O.S. maps 78 and 79, starting point: 107044; pick-up point: 122961.

As for any respectable bank robbery, this walk – running the length of the ridge on the eastern flank of Wamphray glen – requires either two cars or a getaway car at the far end. A suitable pick-up point, at the end of the walk, is near Wamphraygate farm.

Heading east out of Moffat along the A708, you turn right down the narrow road signposted 'Moffat 1½ miles'. The walk starts at the bridge over Moffat Water shortly before Craigbeck. Go through the gate on the left, where the Southern Upland Way is signposted. After about three kilometres, you come upon a small house called Craigbeck Hope standing in a forest clearing. The track continues through delightful surroundings, surprisingly reminiscent of the Austrian Tyrol, up to a bridge where Wamphray Water crosses the track.

At this point the Southern Upland Way leads northwards through a forest ride in the direction of the Selcoth Burn, but we turn south following the track as it doubles back on itself out through the forest to the ruins of Garrogill farm at the head of the glen. You then make your way up over some steep, rough ground, through a conifer plantation and up to a forestry track. To the right, the track (which we will eventually take) leads down into Wamphray Glen through the planted slopes of Ewelairs Hill, but for the moment we head left and uphill, on to the bealach between Ewelairs Hill and Cowan Fell.

Once you are standing on the summit of Cowan Fell, the route, which on the way up was obscured by trees, can be clearly made out,

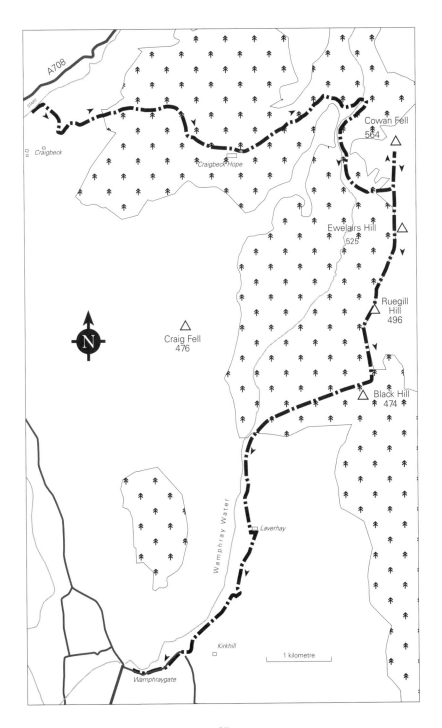

A708

START

Craigbeck

Craigbeck Hope

Cowan Fell
564

Ewelairs Hill
525

Craig Fell
476

Ruegill
Hill
496

Black Hill
474

Wamphray Water

Laverhay

Kirkhill

1 kilometre

Wamphraygate

leading along the top of the ridge, above the trees, over Ewelairs Hill, Ruegill Hill and (now through conifer plantation again) Black Hill.

At Black Hill, follow the forest ride to the west along a ridge, proceed gently down over Kirk Hill and on to the glen above Braefield cottage. The original church or chapel for Wamphray, dating from pre-Reformation times, was at Kirk Hill. Over the west door of the present Wamphray church (not marked on map), which now stands nearer Wamphraygate than the original building, is a finely carved stone salvaged from the original chapel. A one-time minister of Wamphray, John Brown, was a Covenanter who was hunted in these hills. After his eventual capture, he was taken to Edinburgh on horseback, bound hand and foot, for his trial. He was later exiled to Holland.

On the way through the glen, you pass Laverhay farm, by which time the track has turned into a small, surfaced road that leads to Wamphraygate, where you hope that your chauffeur is waiting.

The Dalveen Circuit

This walk of 12.5 km should take about 5 hours. O.S. map 78, starting and finishing point: 878132 (parking).

As parking is prohibited up at the summit of Lowther Hill, you have to leave your car at the bottom of the turn-off to it and walk up. Failing that, you could park in Wanlockhead itself.

Leaving the little village of Wanlockhead, the highest in Scotland, walk up the steep tarmac road which wends its way towards the Civil Aviation Radar Station perched on the summit of Lowther Hill at 725 metres. The views on the way up are impressive, and even more so once you are actually on top of the hills, so it's worth walking right to the summit before beginning the walk proper.

Having admired the view, go back down the road until you reach the sharp bend to the right; there you will be able to make out the path heading off to the south-west down a grassy slope. After passing through a gate, proceed downhill, keeping the fence on your right until you go through another gate to start the climb up on to the ridge on which East Mount Lowther stands. This hill is a recognised viewpoint, that affords magnificent vistas in every direction and is equipped with a stone direction guide to help with peak spotting, erected by members of Wanlockhead Youth Club way back in 1944. On a particularly clear day, you can see not just the Galloway Hills, but the Isle of Man beyond. When I did the walk, the Lake District Hills, across the shimmering Solway Firth, looked almost close enough to touch. The Arran Peaks were in sight beyond the lands of Kyle, and to the north I could see Ben Lomond and the Arrochar 'alps'. As I stood on the summit, I wondered how many of the Youth Club members still go up to view their handiwork.

I descended the western side to rejoin the path which skirts the flanks of East Mount Lowther and then Thirstane Hill. It's a truly delightful path which gently loses height and gives you a view of the Mennock Pass before passing between Thirstane Hill and Threehope Height. Strolling down its grassy slopes, we admired the beauty of the valleys and hills of Nithsdale stretching away ahead of us.

Soon you cross an escarpment with, to the left, a field enclosed by a dyke, and find yourself down in the valley at Auchenlone Burn. The path climbs out of the depths and on over to Coshogle. Another path, the Dempster Road, strikes off to the right towards Glenim. Leave the path you're on and turn to the south-east, keeping Auchenlone Burn below you but gradually heading downhill. It can be rather tricky here

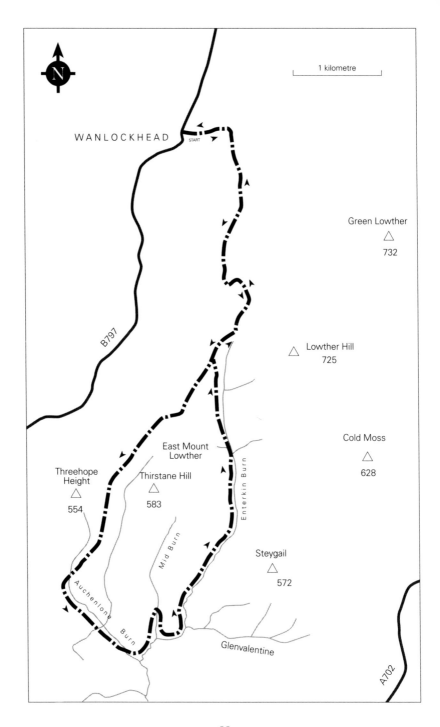

1 kilometre

WANLOCKHEAD START

Green Lowther
△
732

B797

Lowther Hill
△
725

Cold Moss
△
628

East Mount
Lowther

Threehope
Height
△
554

Thirstane Hill
△
583

Enterkin Burn

Mid Burn

Steygail
△
572

Auchenlone Burn

Glenvalentine

A702

as you negotiate the bracken above the burn, but once you have reached the valley floor, you can cross and recross the burn with ease. This is perhaps the most pleasant part of the walk. The bracken-covered hillsides rise steeply on either side. Where Auchenlone Burn is joined by Mid Burn, climb up and over the fence beside the dyke on the left. Above you is a sheep pen, and you walk up with Mid Burn on your right to join the path which crosses the burn and leads on to Enterkin Burn.

Next, take the path that crosses the Enterkin Burn, then runs alongside it on its western bank, heading up the valley to the source on Lowther Hill. (The path is easily recognisable by a line of wooden poles that carry the power line all the way to the top.) From time to time, there are most attractive waterfalls along the way. The eastern side of the valley is punctuated by deep gullies that run into the glen and, as you climb, the huge masses of Steygail and Wether Hill loom overhead.

Soon, you arrive back at your starting point at the gate, and can make your way down to the car.

Craigieburn Wood

4 or 9 kilometres, depending on route taken (*see below*); the longer route takes 3 hours. O.S. map 78, starting point: 124059.

> 'Sweet closes the ev'ning on Craigieburn Wood
> And blithely awakens the morrow;
> But the pride o' the spring in Craigieburn Wood
> Can yield me naught but sorrow.'

Well that's how Burns put it after a visit to the woods way back in about 1789. Lately when I visited it, the evening fell just as sweetly, but I didn't hang around to watch how blithely the morrow awakened.

For those who like signposted walks, this one, established by Forestry Enterprise, certainly has a lot to commend it. In my opinion, it's their best yet. It is not the usual well-pathed, closed-in walk through endless stretches of fir and Sitka. There's a good bit of ascent in this fairly rough walk, and once you have followed the route high up on to the northern slopes of the Moffat Water valley, the views are magnificent.

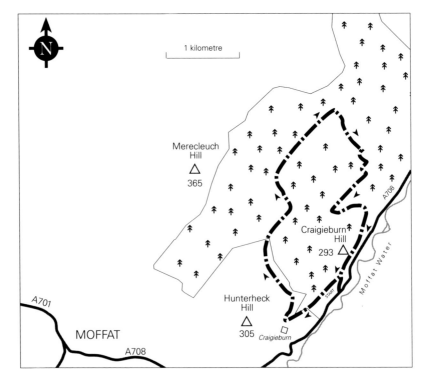

The valley of Moffat Water from Craigbeck.

At the entrance to Craigieburn Wood on the Moffat/Selkirk road (A708), just east of Waterside, two walks are signposted: the Red route, which is 4 kilometres long, and the Yellow route, which is 9 kilometres. Both go round in a loop so that you end up where you began.

We chose the longer, and decided to walk it clockwise, turning off left uphill through the trees. Initially both routes follow the same course. Soon we left the trees behind us and came into the open, skirting the forest and gaining height as we walked. Now we were rewarded with views down Annandale, and then just below us, we glimpsed Craigieburn House nestling in the lea of the hill. This was one of the places chosen by Burns for overnight stops as he journeyed to and from Edinburgh to visit his 'Clarinda' and hob-nob with Edinburgh's aristocracy and literati. Here he penned a few inconsequential lines which indicated that he and his hosts had imbibed fairly well on one night in particular.

Craigieburn was also the birthplace of Jean Lorimer, the 'Chloris' to whom Burns addressed several poems, including one which refers to her as the 'Lassie wi' the lint-white locks'. (You are quite relieved when he refers in other poems to her flaxen hair – the term 'lint-white' conjures up pictures of some white-haired old biddy.)

Jean was the daughter of William Lorimer who was tenant at Kemmishall and a great friend of Robert Burns during his days at Ellisland. Despite his passionate verses to Jean, Burns was seemingly keen that she should marry a fellow exciseman. Typical of her sex, she ignored his advice, married a ne'er-do-weel farmer and had a pretty unhappy marriage. She now lies buried in some Edinburgh cemetery.

Today it is worth visiting Craigieburn for reasons other than Robert Burns's connections with the place. For the nursery that has become established here holds the national collection of *Meconopsis*, or the Himalayan Poppy, the genus that includes the spectacular blue poppies. Not only has the owner been out to the Himalayas to collect these beautiful rare plants, but she has done much to make the gardens at Craigieburn most attractive for visitors.

The view of Craigieburn quickly disappeared behind us as we climbed up round the edge of the woods. Over to our left, views of Upper Annandale opened up. Eventually, after just over a mile, the Yellow route parts company with the Red, which goes straight on. The Yellow route leads ever higher with the ground becoming rougher underfoot, until you are facing up Moffat Water looking over towards Yarrow to the east. And just when you think you may indeed end up in Yarrow, the path leads you gently down by a series of steps cut into the hillside with a rather dodgy-seeming handrail back towards the valley and the main track back to where you started.

To me, the installation of the bench on the descent is the *pièce de résistance* of the whole walk. Whoever placed that seat there must truly have had a heart, as well as an eye, for beauty. For here one can sit at height and look out over a rich patchwork of fir and larch into a view that would be hard to match anywhere. 'Sweet closes the ev'ning on Craigieburn Wood' certainly seemed apt. Before us, the late sun's light carved out Moffat Water's southern hills in breathtaking relief, while to our right Annandale stretched hazily away towards the Solway. It's well worth lingering awhile, before going steeply on down to complete the walk.

Forest Enterprise is to be congratulated on the work carried out to open up their forests to walkers and the way in which the walks have been planned. It's just a pity that our forests keep being sold off piece-meal to all callers at the backdoor. Let's hope that all this good work has not been in vain and that the public are not denied access when the forests, like all the rest of the silverware, vanish into private hands. Recent developments in Upper Nithsdale have a lot of people worried – and quite rightly so.

November's sky is chill and drear,
November's leaf is red and sear.

Sir Walter Scott, *Marmion*

Saddle Yoke

This 13.5 km walk should take about 5 hours. O.S. map 78, starting point: 147098.

Saddle Yoke, for me at least, is one of the most impressive of all the Moffat Hills, its steep flanks rising to a narrow ridge that in turn culminates in the dramatic summit.

In many ways it reminds me of Cat Bells, which stands high above Derwent Water, in Borrowdale. Just as the ridge of Cat Bells carries you at height over Maiden Moor and on to the slopes of Dale Head, so if you follow the ridge of Saddle Yoke high above Black Hope glen, you find yourself in an area of desolate peat hags approaching Hartfell Rig and Hart Fell.

This walk is a variation of the one through Hart Fell and back by the Craigs which is the first in this book. You begin on the A708 at the foot of Black Hope glen, near Capplegill, gradually gain height, climbing up the steep slopes at its head; from here it is only a short walk to the trig point on Hart Fell.

Last time I did it, I was very fortunate with the weather. It was cold, but there was not a cloud in the sky, and a sharp frost had made the ground hard and clean underfoot.

As I made my way up Black Hope glen, sheltered by the steep hills on either side, I cursed the fact that I had put on my thermals, for I was already working up a fair head of steam. One by one, articles of clothing were discarded, until I was climbing in my shirtsleeves.

When I reached the summit plateau of Hart Fell, however, I emerged into another world, and was abruptly reminded of the fact that at 800 metres the temperature is said to be six degrees lower than at sea level. A chill wind cut through my shirt like an icy knife, and my face and ears were straightaway numbed with cold. Clothing was rapidly replaced, as I piled on everything except the spare jersey in my pack. Soon warmth began to return, and I felt just fine.

Lying in the biel of the meagre shelter on Hart Fell I ate my

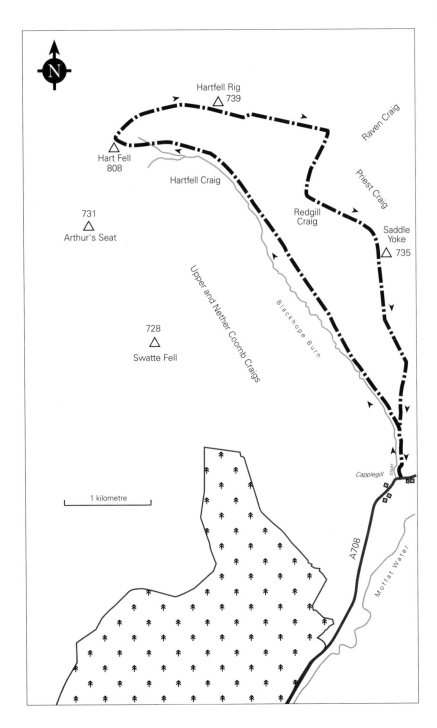

N

Hartfell Rig
△ 739

Raven Craig

Hart Fell
808

Hartfell Craig

Priest Craig

731
△
Arthur's Seat

Redgill
Craig

Saddle
Yoke
△ 735

Upper and Nether Coomb Craigs

Blackhope Burn

728
△
Swatte Fell

1 kilometre

START

Capplegill

A708

Moffat Water

104

Saddle Yoke, White Coomb and Carrifran in winter mantle.

sandwiches and gulped down some warming tea. As I crouched, I was in no doubt that winter had arrived in the hills.

Having reached the summit, follow the fence north-east over Hartfell Rig, until it turns sharply southwards at the edge of Rotten Bottom. After this point you have to cross an area of rough, (usually) wet ground keeping Raven Craig and Priest Craig to your left. Climb the ridge of Saddle Yoke. To get the best out of the ridge walk, it's a good idea to keep to the edge (though never if there is any snow about). Make sure you climb over Redgill Craig on the way; from here there is a fine view down into Black Hope glen.

Days spent walking over hills clad in a mantle of crisp snow are gems indeed, and because I did not have to tend sheep on them, I selfishly rejoiced. Anyone who stows away their rucksack and boots at the onset of winter is leaving the table before the coffee and liqueurs are served.

As I dropped down from the steep end of Saddle Yoke, dusk was beginning to creep stealthily up Moffat Water. Smoke from a nearby shepherd's cottage climbed lazily into the clear winter sky, as the frost hardened its grip for yet another night. A feeling of tranquillity pervaded the valley as darkness set in, and I rejoined the road close to where I had set off.

The Three Burns

The time for this 12.5-kilometre walk is 4 hours (which gets you back to the main road) plus the time it takes to walk just under 2 kilometres back to where your car has been parked (near Capplegill). O.S. map 79, starting point: 147098.

The three burns, Blackhope, Whirly Gill and Carrifran, form the route for an exciting walk through some of the wildest territory in Moffatdale.

A snell wind blew from the east, its breath chilled by the snow-clad tops, as I parked near Blackshope cottage on the Moffat to Selkirk road

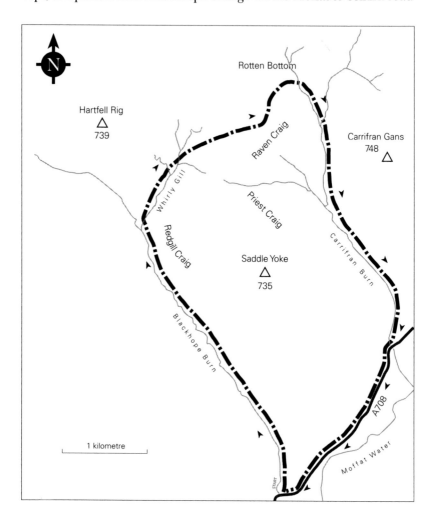

(A708). The numbing wind in my face, as I headed up the track into Black Hope glen, told me that winter had arrived early this year. However it was clear overhead, and the snow on the tops of Hart Fell and Hartfell Rig glistened in the sun.

My intention was to follow the Blackhope Burn up to where the Whirly Gill burn rushes out of the steep-sided gully from the direction of Rotten Bottom. I would then return to the main road by following the Carrifran Burn out, more or less circumnavigating the mass of Saddle Yoke. This is not a very long walk in terms of distance but it can be quite demanding in winter.

On the way up the glen I spoke with Capplegill's head shepherd as he put out food supplements for the ewes. It was an arduous task that involved crossing and recrossing the burn. The ewes were being given a high-vitamin feed so that they would be looking their best when they met the 'gents' later that month.

At about 450 metres I came on soft, powdery snow and gingerly picked my way over the slippery boulders to cross Whirly Gill as it entered Black Hope glen. The distinctive 'churk-churk' of the solitary raven that wheeled above my head sounded loud in the snowy calm. I wondered if it was the same one I had seen in exactly this spot a week before.

Having crossed the Gill, I followed its north bank up through the bealach between Hartfell Rig and Saddle Yoke. The snow was deeper now and it was quite hard going as the climb steepened. A cluster of wild goats stood on the heights gazing down at me, no doubt wondering about the sanity of *Homo sapiens.*

Where the Gill forks, I stopped and took a compass bearing on the corner of the fence at Rotten Bottom. I was now heading more-or-less north-east and the going had become really tough – a wilderness of peat hags.

I was suddenly aware of a dark shape silhouetted against the sky on my right. Peering at me from behind a peat hag was the outline of a deer's head, its ears standing up at the alert. We studied each other for several minutes, and then it was off in a flurry of powdery snow, gliding effortlessly over the rough ground in the direction of Saddle Yoke. I'm pretty sure it was a Sika – from its very dark coat and its height of about four feet. Unlike the more gregarious Red Deer, it was alone, which is typical of the species. The Sika is a native of Asia, and the animals around Tweedsmuir are descendants of deer that originally escaped from captivity. They seem to be attracted to the wet moorland and wooded shelter in the area and have been spreading down into Moffatdale, albeit in small numbers.

Standing at the corner of the fence, we were now on the edge of the notorious Rotten Bottom – an area of sodden wet marsh. Just over a mile away to the north-west lies Gameshope Loch, at over 550 metres the highest in the Southern Uplands, and traditionally said to have connections with Merlin, the last Druid and an adviser to King Arthur. Be that as it may, the area was certainly important in Covenanting times. Beneath the ground between Gameshope Loch and Talla, there are supposed to be underground caverns that were reached through small openings above ground and served as hiding places for Covenanters. I have been told that you can come upon one of these entrances by accident, but it is well-nigh impossible to find it again. Fugitives holed up in this area for some time often became quite desperate with hunger, and shepherds turned a blind eye when the odd sheep disappeared; it was easier to let them kill a lamb than to give spare food from their own meagre larders.

I plunged down through the snow, following the fence and, keeping well clear of the cliffs on Raven Craig, headed towards Firthhope Rig. Instead of following the fence once it begins to climb up the slopes, wend your way steeply down into Carrifran glen. As you follow the Carrifran Burn you will see its other source coming down off Carrifran Gans in a pretty spectacular waterfall. Further along the burn you pick up a path which becomes more defined the further down the valley you go and finally brings you out on to the main road at Carrifran cottage about two kilometres from the car.

DECEMBER

The sun, that brief December day,
Rose cheerless over hills of gray,
And darkly circled, gave at noon
A sadder light than warming soon.

J.C. Whittier, 'Snow Bound'

The Crown of Scotland

This 15-kilometre walk should take just under 4 hours. O.S. map 78, starting point: 056127.

Having driven a few kilometres north out of Moffat along the Edinburgh road (A701), we parked the car on the right-hand side of the road – at the entrance to a forest ride, with the vast amphitheatre of the Devil's Beef Tub dropping away below us.

The name of this famous spot is well-earned, for it was an ideal place for the reivers to hide cattle stolen from across the border. Here the beasts were well penned in and hidden from the prying eyes of the pursuing English.

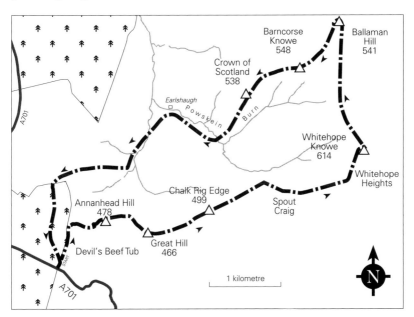

Winter comes to Earlshaugh.

Just off the main road, below the summit, visitors can read the inscription on a monument that tells of the covenanter who was shot on the slopes of Great Hill by dragoons. I can well imagine the panic and fear of the fugitive as he scrambled breathlessly up the steep slopes in a desperate attempt to escape. His flight was brought to an abrupt end by a dragoon's musket shot.

This walk is a circuit of the tops that divide Tweedsmuir from the narrow head of Annandale. On a fine day it can reward one with the best view in the Southern Uplands.

After going through the gate, leave the ride immediately and instead strike up the hill, following the fence up the side of the conifer plantation. Soon you reach the trig point on Annanhead Hill. From here strike a little south from the fence, and head up on to Great Hill. It's worth pausing to admire the scenery and gaze down into the Tub with the infant Annan springing from its floor. Every time I stand here, looking southwards towards the Solway, I'm more than ever convinced that Annandale is the most beautiful valley in the south of Scotland – a truly wonderful place in which to live.

Return to the fence (which marks the boundary between Dumfries & Galloway and Borders Region) and follow the undulating terrain up over Chalk Rig Edge. From here you scramble down, then up again to the top of Spout Craig. About here the fence suddenly comes to an end, as if it had got tired of climbing up and down along the edge of the Tub.

My next stop on the walk is Whitehope Knowe, at 614 metres. Here the ground plunges precipitously to the valley floor, before rising again in the shape of the huge mass of Hart Fell to the south-east. To the north you can see Fruid Reservoir and to the north-nor'west the small cairn on top of Ballaman Hill – our next objective, before Barncorse Knowe. Keep to the high ground, and climb up to the summit of the surprisingly grandly named Crown of Scotland. Looking back, you can trace the route you have come, right along the edge of the Beef Tub.

Down to the west lies the now-deserted farm of Earlshaugh; its roof has fallen in and all that remains is a gaunt shell. It was probably last occupied in the late 'twenties or early 'thirties. Farming out here must have been a very lonely existence, with home three miles down a rough track from the nearest main road. Our route, however, leads south here, and the next landmark is the precariously narrow footbridge over the Powskein Burn, reached across a short stretch of rough ground. Following the burn down towards Earlshaugh, I was struck by how impressive it looked, surging through two miniature ravines, on its way to join Cor Water.

After passing the steading, cross the bridge spanning Cor Water and follow the track out past the sheep pens and back towards the forest ride gate. On reaching the gate, look over towards Tweedshaws on the A701. The old road to Edinburgh followed the forest ride down the track you see today out to Tweedshaws farm. This was originally an inn and a point where horse-drawn carriages, notably the Royal Mail Coach journeying between Edinburgh and London, took on fresh steeds. You can still see the stables at the rear of the building. Walk twenty or so paces down the track towards Tweedshaws and to your left-hand side you will see a small, square, sandstone block that marks the spot where James McGeorge's body was found. He was the guard, who, with the driver, John Goodfellow, set out with the mail coach from Moffat to Edinburgh during a fierce snowstorm in February 1831. The coach got stuck, and the two struggled on through the deep snow on foot, taking the mail bags with them, eventually to collapse and die in the snow. It is in this area that at dusk you may well catch sight of short-eared owls gliding silently overhead.

The winter snow lies deep near Earlshaugh.

The monument to the two dead mailmen beside the A701.

Swatte Fell and Black Hope from Archbank Spa

This 19-kilometre walk takes about 4½ hours. O.S. map 78, starting and finishing point: 092073.

When Rachel Whyteford discovered the sulphureous springs bubbling out of the ground near Archbank just above the wee town of Moffat way back in 1633, she can have had little notion of what she was starting. For the strong-smellling water bubbling out of the hillside at her feet was eventually to put Moffat firmly on the map. Along with the nearby springs at Hartfell and Garpol, they were to attract thousands of visitors to this small town nestling among the hills of Annandale.

Moffat's popularity as a spa town really got going in the late 18th and early 19th centuries when the physicians of Edinburgh began to recommend that their patients visit the springs and bathe in their waters, as well as drinking repulsively large quantities of it. The worthy doctors of Auld Reekie recommended it for all manner of ailments – from gout to chest ailments – in fact, pretty much everything except in-growing toe nails.

At Archbank a building was erected over the two springs and a grand function room, complete with verandah, was built nearby. From early morning the road up from the town to Archbank would be thronged with people walking up to the Spa, threading their way out between a procession of charabancs. The water was piped all the way down to the town to heated baths in the building that now houses the Town Hall. Meanwhile, in Moffat itself, hotels sprang up to accommodate the visitors.

There are two springs at the source of the Well Burn. Water from the top one was piped down into the town to be used as bath water. The bottom spring contained more sulphur and other elements and was drunk by the patients. Many years ago, I risked a tiny sip of the waters and, from what I tasted, I would imagine one would quickly stop worrying about whatever ailed you and start worrying about the effects of the water. One can still see the two water spouts, but all that remains of the pipeline down to the town is the odd bit of concrete where inspection covers used to be.

So the Moffat Well beyond Archbank is the starting point for our walk. If you're lucky enough to get as fine a day as I had, you should be rewarded with some splendid views. Park your car in the car park at the well, and set off through the gate following the path up on to the hill. The day I was there, a large dog fox nonchalantly crossed my path further up the hill before disappearing into the bracken. The day

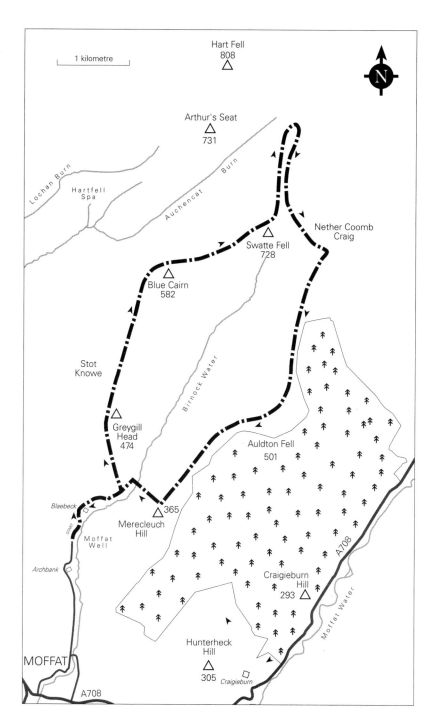

1 kilometre

Hart Fell
808

Arthur's Seat
731

Lochan Burn

Hartfell
Spa

Auchencat Burn

Nether Coomb
Craig

Swatte Fell
728

Blue Cairn
582

Stot
Knowe

Birnock Water

Greygill
Head
474

Auldton Fell
501

Blaebeck

365

Merecleuch
Hill

Moffat
Well

A708

Archbank

Craigieburn
Hill
293

Moffat Water

MOFFAT

Hunterheck
Hill

305   Craigieburn

A708

promised well with only odd patches of mist hanging over the upper slopes of Arthur's Seat and Hart Fell.

After passing the shepherd's house at Blaebeck, you come to a fork. Ignore the path that heads off to the left and take the one that goes on through the gate. After a short distance, leave the path, striking left up the hillside along a grassy path up to and along the ridge. This takes you nicely up on to Greygill Head. Go right up to the cairn, pick up the fence and follow it, keeping it to your right, heading towards Blue Cairn.

Gradually gaining height, walk over Stot Knowe, still with the fence and dyke on your right: on the approach to Blue Cairn, leave the fence where it 'dog-legs' to the right, and keep straight on for the summit. On the day I was there, the mist rolled back at this point, and I was presented with a fine view up to the north west of the Beef Tub complete with the ridge at its head. Finally, as I climbed on to the summmit of Swatte Fell, the great mass of Hart Fell shook off its enveloping cover and loomed up to my left – I pressed on, aiming for Black Hope glen.

Standing on the peak directly above Falcon Craig, I could hardly believe my good luck – the whole of Black Hope glen, Saddle Yoke, Carrifran and White Coomb were bathed in brilliant sunshine. I looked directly across the valley to Whirly Gill on its left and saw the ridge on which I stood silhouetted in shadow on the other side of the glen. On the hillside opposite I could make out every contour of my proposed route. It brought home to me just how insignificant I was in relation to my surroundings.

Wanting to savour the ridge, I followed the edge of the craigs and coombs south as far as the cairn at Nether Coomb Craig; the two dogs and I stopped on the way along for our lunch in the sheltered neck of a gully. At the cairn, I decided to head across the open hillside towards the corner of the forest to the south. The mist looked as if it might sweep in again, so I took a compass reading and set off in a south westerly direction. Picking up the fence at the edge of the forest, I turned south and followed it round and up over Auldton Fell. It's quite rough going, so, unless it's very dry weather, don't attempt to take a short cut in the open on to the top – you'll find yourself in the midst of very boggy ground.

I soon picked up a faint track along the edge of the hill which took me downhill towards a dyke radiating out from the forest just before the summit of Merecleuch Hill. Having followed the dyke down towards Birnock Water, I had the choice of jumping across the burn or taking my chances on a very narrow, precarious-looking bridge – I chose the former. My route then took me up to the forestry track and back to Blaebeck and the Well.

There used to be a custodian's cottage just opposite the Well. It has now been converted into a very attractive bungalow, and I had a pleasant chat with its present owner. Here was a man highly content with both his abode and his surroundings. And so he should be – he must have the finest view in Annandale.

Hart Fell by Whirly Gill

A 15-kilometre walk that takes about just over 5 hours to complete. O.S. map 79, starting and finishing point: 147098.

'All things are artificial; for nature is the art of God'. Thus wrote Thomas Browne, way back in the seventeenth century. With today's concerns about conservation in mind, his words still seem pretty relevant. Suddenly, over the last few years, we seem to have begun to wake up to the fact that we are killing off our forests with acid rain, polluting our seas with chemicals and sewage and frying ourselves by exposure to ultra-violet rays through an ozone layer in which we ourselves have poked a hole.

Speaking personally, it's humanity's interference with nature in the hills that has me worried. When things artificial are introduced into a natural environment, they stick out like a sore thumb. I'm thinking, for example, of the tourist centres at Ben Lawers and Glencoe. Did that philanthropist, Percy Unna, have such monstrosities in mind when in the 1930s he put up a large amount of money in order to protect the Glen and its surrounding mountains? I don't think so. The only consolation is that there are moves to shift the information centre out of Glencoe. All this carping may sound a bit selfish, but we have only one chance to preserve nature.

A walk like this one, up on to Hart Fell by Whirly Gill, drives all such sombre thoughts from one's mind. The day I did it, the sky was clear, the air was cold and up on the tops a crisp inch of snow lay about – ideal conditions for a winter walk.

Leave the car at Blackshope cottage on the Moffat to Selkirk road (O.S. map 78, grid ref. 146098). Keeping to the right-hand side of Blackhope Burn, walk up the glen. This part of the walk, following the burn, can be a pretty glaurie affair, though the day we were there, the ground was firm and frosty underfoot. However, the owner of Capplegill has since driven a track up Black Hope glen nearly as far as Whirly Gill, which makes the going somewhat easier.

Our intention was to swing up into the cleft on our right between Redgill Craig and Saddle Craigs where Whirly Gill comes rushing out through the rocks to join Blackhope Burn. The temptation is to stay in the valley as far as Whirly Gill, but we cut uphill short of the Gill, climbing its southern slopes and turning into the cleft just beneath the screes on Redgill. It's drier this way, and you don't have such a difficult climb all the way from the valley up Whirly Gill. Crossing Whirly Gill in spate can be hazardous, so we decided to keep to its

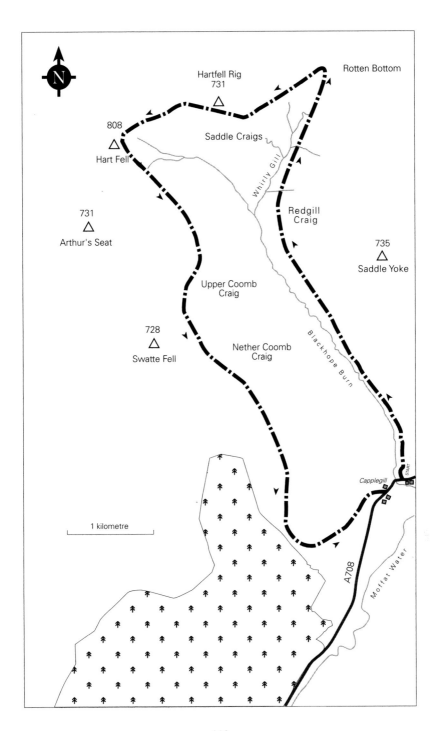

N

Hartfell Rig
731

Rotten Bottom

808

Hart Fell

Saddle Craigs

Whirly Gill

731

Arthur's Seat

Redgill
Craig

735

Saddle Yoke

Upper Coomb
Craig

728

Swatte Fell

Nether Coomb
Craig

Blackhope Burn

START

Capplegill

1 kilometre

A708

Moffat Water

southern bank. Not far along, we came upon a wild goat and her kid grazing on the opposite bank. We all studied each other at close quarters – the goats safe in the knowledge that the burn lay between us.

From here it's a steep pull up north-east over the bealach following the left-hand fork of Whirly Gill back up the burn as it flows out through the peat hags. It can be pretty wet here but we found the ground frozen. We joined the fence a few hundred metres south-west of its corner at Rotten Bottom and followed it up the slopes of Hartfell Rig. It's an easy gradient and eventually takes you on to Hart Fell itself. Stop on the way up and admire the fine views of the hills of Tweedsmuir and Fruid Reservoir lying beneath you to the north.

Leaving Hart Fell summit we dropped down to the south-east over Hartfell Craig, facing into a bright winter sun and picking our way carefully along the edge of the ridge above Black Hope glen. The way to experience the true magnificence of this high ridge in winter is to take the path along the very edge – following it round the coombs. However this should be done only with great care and knowledge of the area, and if you are a walker with experience of winter conditions. There is a treacherous phenomenen called cornicing, where a snow overhang can look perilously like solid ground from above. At least one experienced climber in the last few years has had a fatal accident in this area when he stepped through a cornice to his death. Looking south, we could make out the Lake District Hills; to the east were the Pennines and to their left the murky outline of the Eildons.

At the far end of the ridge, at Capplegill farm, the descent can be pretty difficult. It's extremely steep and, especially in winter, can be tricky. I suggest that you follow the ridge as far out to its western end as possible and descend to the edge of the wood, then follow its eastern edge, near Roundstonefoot Burn, downhill. About half a kilometre from the main road a path leads off to the left and down to Capplegill farm, just 25 metres from Blackshope cottage.

Appendices

Glossary

Scattered through the book are a few Scots words that may be unfamiliar to those not versed in the vocabulary. So here are a few definitions to ease comprehension:

abune	above
bealach	a narrow mountain pass
biel	place giving refuge or shelter
bothy	rough hut used as temporary accommodation, for example, by shepherds, fishermen, walkers
coorie doon	stoop or crouch down
couthie	(of people) friendly, sociable; (of places) comfortable, snug
drouthy	thirsty
glaurie	muddy, dirty
hags	a hillock of firmer ground in a bog
howf	shelter
kenspeckle	conspicuous
loaning	grassy track
reive	steal, plunder
snell	(of weather) biting, bitter, severe
steading	farm building
steg	stride
well-kent	familiar
whaup	curlew

What's in a Name?

It always makes walks more interesting if you can find the derivation of the names of the hills over which you have been clambering. In a way, it's a bit like knowing an old friend's past.

Up in the north of Scotland, it's usually a matter of translating from the Gaelic, and over in Galloway many of the hills have names that are Gaelic in origin. The sources of hill names in the borders are often more obscure; some of the more readily intelligible involve Scots dialect. A number are named for their appearance: White Coomb, Blue Cairn, White Shank, Green Law, Black Knowe Head, Scaw'd [dappled] Law and Faugh [pale red] Hill. Some are called after animals: Foal Burn, Ewe Gair, Ewe Hill, Lamb Hill and Wedder Law.

My favourites are those which defy derivation: Muckle Knees, Nickies Knowe, Andrewhinney Hill and Herman Law. I prefer to remain in blissful ignorance, imagining one shepherd on the hillside above Megget blessed with especially big knees, and another, of German origin, walking the Bodesbeck Ridge.

The following is a selection of hill names around Moffat and their meanings:

Andrewhinney Hill
'Whinney' could refer to whins (Scots for gorse bushes); Andrew may have been a local farmer or shepherd.

Arthur's Seat
A shoulder of Hart Fell thought to have connections with King Arthur and Merlin.

Barry Grain Rig
'Grain' means a long stream; 'rig' means ridge.

Beacon Hill
The site of a bonfire lit as a beacon, possibly to warn of impending attacks by the English.

Bell Craig
'Bell' means lump; 'craig' means crag.

Broadlaw
'Law' means hill.

Capel Fell
Used in southern Scotland and the Lake District, 'fell' is a word of Norse origin meaning hill. 'Capell' means a work- or cart-horse.

Carrifran Gans
'Gans' means jaws in Scots.

Cramalt Craig.
'Alt' is Gaelic for burn or stream; 'cram-alt' means a crooked stream.

Crown of Scotland
I am baffled as to why this relatively modest hill should have such a grand title, though one theory has it that the followers of Robert the Bruce thought that its outline resembled a crown and took this as a good omen as they marched to Scone for his coronation.

Dollar Law
'Law' means hill.

Devil's Beef Tub
Named for its function as an ideal place into which to drive stolen cattle. This steep-sided natural corral has only one way in and out and was therefore extremely easy to guard.

Dun Law
'Dun' means light-coloured in Scots; 'law' means hill.

Earl's Haugh
Possibly named after a local landowner (the Earl of Annandale?), or because of its proximity to the Crown of Scotland; 'haugh' means a flat piece of land.

Faugh Hill
'Faugh' means pale red in Scots.

Firthyhope Rig
'Rig' is a steep-sided ridge.

Green Lowther
Green refers to this hill's grassy slopes.

Hart Fell
Reputed to be the home of Merlin, who, on occasion, could assume the shape of a hart or deer.

Knockenhair
Knoll or hilltop where a watch was kept for interlopers or attackers.

Lochurd Hill
'Ord' or 'urd' means a steep, rounded hill.

Midge Hill
Possibly named after the scourge of Western Scotland – a nasty wee blood-sucking insect.

Molls Cleuch Dod
'Dod' is a bare hill; 'cleuch' or 'cleugh' can mean either a gorge or ravine (e.g. Thick Cleuch near Wedder Law) or a cliff (e.g. Donald's Cleuch Head).

Nickies Knowe
'Knowe' is a lot bigger than an English knoll (small, rounded hilltop).

Peat Law
Peat was probably cut from these slopes at some time; 'law' means hill.

Saddle Yoke
Named because of its similarity to a horse's saddle.

Scaw'd Law
'Scaw'd' means dappled; 'law', as before, means hill.

Steygail Hill
'Stey' means steep, and 'gail' means a crack.

Watch Hill, **Watch Knowe** and **Watchman's Brae**
All would have been used as look-out points during the Reiving and Covenanting times.

Wedder Law
A wedder is a young, castrated male lamb.

White Coomb
A coomb is a cleft in the hills.

Flora and Fauna

The hills around Moffat are ideal territory for the hillwalker with an interest in birdlife. In addition to the species which breed locally, one can spot many interesting migrants.

Unfortunately since the reduction in sheep stocks, the raven population has dwindled somewhat, although I hear it is now beginning to recover. However, thanks to local vigilance, the peregrine falcon survives in reasonable numbers. A walk over heather-clad slopes will still often make a red or black grouse break cover and fly off with its characteristic strident cackle.

Little Loch Skeen may no longer be the haunt of the Golden Eagle, but it is at times home to a large colony of black-headed gulls, and the golden eagle and osprey have both been seen in the hills. A local ornithologist, Jock Dicerbo, reports having spotted snow bunting, osprey, a golden eagle and a little owl, all within the space of two hours. To whet your appetite, here is a list of birds that have been seen in this area, among them breeding species, winter visitors and passing migrants:

blackbird, buzzard, carrion crow, chaffinch, cuckoo, curlew (known locally as a whaup), dipper, dunlin, fieldfare, golden eagle, golden plover, red grouse, black grouse, blackheaded gull, common gull, lesser blackbacked gull, hen harrier, heron, kestrel, meadow pipit, merlin, osprey, little owl, long-eared owl, short-eared owl, oystercatcher, peregrine falcon, redwing, ring ouzel, raven, skylark, snow bunting, songthrush, stonechat, grey wagtail, wheatear, whinchat and wren.

The most common species of deer seen in these hills is the roe deer. Red deer come into the area only in relatively small numbers and are seen mainly further to the west. Fallow deer are on the increase at lower levels, and the sika, found nearer Tweedsmuir, is gradually moving south. In winter, both the stoat and the mountain hare can be seen sporting their winter coats.

The humble vole is the key to the ecology of the hills. At the moment, its numbers are high, ensuring an ample food supply for foxes, weasels and owls, among other predators.

The rabbit population is on the increase and steadily moving higher up the hill, providing a valuable source of food for various predators, in particular, the buzzard, whose numbers are also growing steadily.

Nobody's friend, the adder, is seldom found east of the M74.

The wildflowers listed below have been spotted and pointed out to me by my wife, Maureen, usually just as I was about to stand on them. Of this collection, perhaps the dwarf cornel deserves a special mention as it is rare to find it in our hills. The only other location where I have seen it was on the slopes of Ben Loyal in Sutherland. You may well be able to add more to this list during your hill wanderings, but remember that it is an offence to pick certain species of wildflowers. Among the plants to be found are:

alpine mouse-ear chickweed, butterwort, cloudberry, cotton grass, cow-wheat, cranesbill, dwarf cornel, eyebright, grass of Parnassus, heath bedstraw, lady's mantle, marsh marigold (known locally as butter blobs), marsh orchid, marsh violet, meadow rue, milkwort, mountain everlasting, ragged robin, rose-root, starry saxifrage, sundew, thyme, tormentil.

Moffat Mountain Rescue Team

Moffat Mountain Rescue Team was founded in the spring of 1969. Before its establishment, lost or injured walkers and climbers depended on the good offices of local shepherds, gamekeepers, hillwalkers and the local doctor. A fatal accident at the Grey Mare's Tail involving a young Edinburgh schoolboy in February 1969 underlined the need for a dedicated rescue service. A meeting was convened in Moffat by the late Dr Hugh Sinclair, a band of volunteers formed and then grew, and the team was born.

At first, equipment was scarce, but this was more than compensated for by a wealth of goodwill and enthusiasm. A heavy wooden stretcher, capable of being towed as a sledge, was constructed, and ground anchors fashioned by the local blacksmith. Shepherd's boots, 'wellies', deer stalkers and belted raincoats were the order of the day. Fund-raising started, and the townsfolk responded magnificently.

Today, the people of Moffat consider the team very much their own. They show a keen interest in its activities and, in common with others in the area and from further afield, still support it by generous donations. For two things have remained constant in the thirty years of the team's existence. The members are still all unpaid volunteers, and the team depends exclusively on donations from the public and professional support from the police.

Over the years, M.M.R.T. has been involved in many searches and rescues throughout the Southern Uplands and in the surrounding countryside, sometimes of a non-hill nature. Perhaps the most notable of these was the search for victims of the tragic Pan Am incident at Lockerbie. More recently, motorists stranded on a snow-bound M74 were brought down to safety; others were supplied by the team with food while they waited.

Today's team boasts two doctors, and its equipment is a far cry from that of the old days. The wooden stretcher has long since been replaced by a number of lightweight MacInnes models, Vibrams have taken over from wellingtons, and Goretex has supplanted the old belted raincoat. A four-wheel drive vehicle gets members to their target area fast, and the presence of one or two female members adds to the balance of the team.

The tradition and team spirit are still strong. A founder member, the late Tom Murray, was awarded the B.E.M. and the Royal Humane Society Medal for rescues. Father and son members are not uncommon, and today's team leader, Neil Sutherland, started 'serving his time' as a sixteen-year-old founder member.

If any readers feel they would like to contribute to team funds, donations can be sent to: The Treasurer, Moffat Mountain Rescue Team, Covesea, Ballplay Road, Moffat, Dumfriesshire.